The Mysterious  & Unknown

Werewolves

by Stuart A. Kallen

ReferencePoint Press®

San Diego, CA

For more information, contact:
ReferencePoint Press, Inc.
PO Box 27779
San Diego, CA 92198
www.ReferencePointPress.com

Picture credits:
Cover: Dreamstime
iStockphoto.com: 6, 8, 11, 34, 36, 40, 77
Landov: 9, 90
North Wind: 28, 32, 52, 57
Photofest: 71
Photoshot: 14, 21, 49, 63, 66, 82

Series design and book layout:
Amy Stirnkorb

LIBRARY OF CONGRESS CATALOGING-IN-PUBLICATION DATA

Kallen, Stuart A., 1955-
  Werewolves / by Stuart A. Kallen.
     p. cm. -- (Mysterious & unknown)
  Includes bibliographical references and index.
  ISBN-13: 978-1-60152-097-5 (hardback)
  ISBN-10: 1-60152-097-2 (hardback)
  1. Werewolves--Juvenile literature. I. Title.
  GR830.W4K35 2009

  398.24'54--dc22

                                                    2009027097

CONTENTS

FOREWORD

"**Strange is our situation here upon earth.**"
—*Albert Einstein*

Since the beginning of recorded history, people have been perplexed, fascinated, and even terrified by events that defy explanation. While science has demystified many of these events, such as volcanic eruptions and lunar eclipses, some remain outside the scope of the provable. Do UFOs exist? Are people abducted by aliens? Can some people see into the future? These questions and many more continue to puzzle, intrigue, and confound despite the enormous advances of modern science and technology.

It is these questions, phenomena, and oddities that Reference-Point Press's *The Mysterious & Unknown* series is committed to exploring. Each volume examines historical and anecdotal evidence as well as the most recent theories surrounding the topic in debate. Fascinating primary source quotes from scientists, experts, and eyewitnesses as well as in-depth sidebars further inform the text. Full-color illustrations and photos add to each book's visual appeal. Finally, source notes, a bibliography, and a thorough index provide further reference and research support. Whether for research or the curious reader, *The Mysterious & Unknown* series is certain to satisfy those fascinated by the unexplained.

Introduction

Horror in the Moonlight

S ince ancient times people have referred to the period between midnight and 3:00 A.M. as the "witching hour." This refers to the time of night when supernatural shape-shifters are said to transform from human beings into ferocious beasts. While innocent people sleep, witches, wizards, and others assume the traits of animals. Some fly through the night like bats, others slink through the dark like cats. But among the most fearful of shape-shifters are those who morph into the dreaded beast known as the werewolf. Part human, part canine, a werewolf combines the cunning brain of a man with the heightened senses, stamina, and strength of a starving wolf. The result is a creature with savage bloodlust unfettered by the rules of civilized society. This beast has haunted the nightmares of human beings since the dawn of time.

It is said that werewolves can be created several ways. Some are the target of a black magic spell that turns them into a hairy, drooling, snarling wolf man. Others assume the shape when bitten or scratched by a werewolf. However they are transformed,

Werewolves prowl while innocents sleep. Part human and part canine, these supernatural creatures are said to have heightened senses, immense strength, and menacing eyes.

the human being becomes a beast with the instincts of a predatory wolf.

A Pack of Werewolves

While many doubt the existence of these creatures of the night, numerous werewolf sightings are reported every year. One such report came from northern Vermont in November 2006. A 21-year-old woman named Tonya said she was driving home from work at 3:00 A.M. with a full moon lighting up surrounding fields and forests when she spotted a large animal running alongside her car. It was on 4 legs but was so large that it was able to peer in her window while keeping pace as she drove down the road at about 30 miles per hour (48kph). Tonya describes the unusual sight:

I wasn't scared at first. . . . I was absolutely enthralled with the thing, which didn't resemble any creature outside fiction I've ever seen before. Its large, funny-looking muzzle filled with protruding teeth, its bright and glowing red eyes and the strange way it loped along with me told me quickly it wasn't a human dressed up to play some kind of trick on me or other passersby. For one thing . . . [no] human on its hands and knees could run like this thing did.[1]

"I've never seen a werewolf again, though nothing in this world will make me dispute the fact . . . I've escaped a pack of them on that night."
—Tonya, eyewitness to a pack of werewolves.

Tonya says the creature was a werewolf and it ran beside her car for more than a mile. She was not afraid until she realized that the beast was not alone. It belonged to a pack with two other werewolves working together to force her car to a halt. The beasts darted in front of Tonya's vehicle, slowing down or stopping, forcing her to swerve around them. Finally, Tonya stomped down on the gas pedal and quickly accelerated. As she pulled away, she saw the three werewolves loping down the middle of the road still trying to catch her car.

Tonya told her story to others, but her friends found it hard to believe. Addressing those who doubt her, Tonya says, "I've never seen a werewolf again, though nothing in this world will make me dispute the fact I've not only seen one . . . I've escaped a pack of them on that night."[2]

A full moon creates a forest silhouette, much like the night in 2006 when a 21-year-old woman encountered a pack of werewolves while driving down a quiet road in northern Vermont.

Werewolves in the Movies

The werewolves Tonya encountered ran on 4 legs, similar to those described in ancient tales. This is different from creatures portrayed in movies, which for the most part run on 2 legs like human beings. One of the most renowned werewolf movies, *The Wolf Man*, was released in 1941. It features Lon Chaney Jr. as a mild-mannered Welshman who becomes a rampaging werewolf when the moon is full. His transformations begin after he is bitten by another such beast. *The Wolf Man* established several werewolf traditions that would appear in dozens of movies that followed, from the low-budget 1957 *I Was a Teenage Werewolf*, to the shocking *Ginger Snaps*, released in 2000. Such movies perpetuate the idea that people become werewolves after surviving an attack by another wolf man. This always takes place during a full moon, during which time the victims grow fangs, sprout hair all over their bodies, and begin walking in a gorilla-type lope. These creatures can only be killed by a silver bullet.

While such images are fixed in the public mind, actual tales of werewolf sightings are more varied. With werewolves common to all cultures throughout the world, the beasts are as diverse as the lands where they live. The werewolf is one of the great enigmas of history. Never captured or photographed but often seen, the beast's piercing howls haunt the dreams of humanity and strike fear whenever they are on the prowl.

Actor Lon Chaney Jr. portrayed a werewolf in the 1941 film The Wolf Man. *The mask he wore for the role (pictured) and his portrayal of the creature established an image of werewolves in the public mind.*

CHAPTER 1

The Ancient Beast

In Central America the ancient Aztecs spoke of the *nahual*, a shape-shifting magician that transformed himself into a caninelike beast to perform black magic. In the Philippines stories are told about the *aswang*, a person who turns into a wolf to eat human flesh in the dark of night. In Ethiopia tradition holds that certain sorcerers called *boudas* can change into carnivorous doglike animals called were-hyenas. From China to the United States, similar legends of shape-shifting were-creatures have long been part of the cultural fabric.

While the origins of werewolves are lost to history, human societies have long coexisted with canines such as the wolf, fox, coyote, jackal, and hyena. Around 15,000 years ago humans tamed the gray wolf, or *Canis lupus*, which evolved into the

domesticated dog. However, a fear of wolves remains deep within the human consciousness, and this has been expressed through-out the centuries in werewolf legends.

One of the earliest references to werewolves comes from po-ems carved in stone tablets in ancient Mesopotamia more than 4,000 years ago. *The Epic of Gilgamesh,* which is the oldest known written work on earth, is about King Gilgamesh, who lived on the Euphrates River in what is now Iraq. In *The Epic of Gilgamesh,* the goddess of love, war, and fertility, named Ishtar, wants the king to marry her. However, Gilgamesh refuses. He knows that those she loves—whether they be animals, gods, or men—suffer cruelty and even death at her hands. Gilgamesh recites their fates to Ishtar:

> Listen to me while I tell the tale of your lovers. There was [the harvest god] Tammuz, the lover of your youth, for him you decreed wailing, year after year. You loved the many-colored roller [bird], but still you struck and broke his wing. . . . You have loved the lion, tremendous in strength: seven pits you dug for him. . . . You have loved the stallion magnificent in battle, and for him you decreed the whip and spur. . . . You have loved the shepherd of the flock; he made meal-cake for you day after day, he killed kids [baby goats] for your sake. You struck and turned him into a wolf; now his own herd-boys chase him away, his own hounds worry [bite at] his flanks.[3]

Ishtar's wolf-shepherd was as harmless to humans as most real wolves, easily driven off by herders and sheep dogs. However, the idea of a person becoming a wolf through supernatural means took on a darker tone several centuries later in ancient Greek mythology. The story is told of King Lycaon, who brought a high level of civilization to the Arcadia region of Greece. Lycaon was said to have 50 sons, each of whom founded a city. Lycaon also had one daughter, Callisto, who became the lover of Zeus, the supreme god of the ancient Greeks.

Lycaon wanted to honor Zeus, so he invited him to a special banquet. Hoping to make an impression on the all-powerful god, Lycaon served Zeus a meal containing meat from a roasted human being. Rather than impressing Zeus, the gesture angered him greatly. As punishment, Zeus turned Lycaon into a wolf. Roman poet Ovid describes Lycaon's sudden transformation in the story *Metamorphoses*, written around A.D. 15: "[Lycaon] ran in terror, and reaching the silent fields howled aloud, frustrated of speech. Foaming at the mouth, and greedy as ever for killing, he turned against the sheep, still delighting in blood. His clothes became bristling hair, his arms became legs. He was a wolf, but kept some vestige of his former shape."[4]

Lycaon's name comes from the Greek word *lykos*, meaning "wolf." And the transformation of Lycaon into a wolf gave rise to the word *lycanthropy*. This term describes a person turning into a werewolf either through magical means or as a curse from the gods as punishment for some great offense.

"Dead with Terror"

Werewolves similar to Ovid's King Lycaon continue to resonate in literature throughout the years. In the story *Satyricon*, written by Roman author Petronius around A.D. 60, a former slave, Niceros, describes his encounter with a werewolf. Niceros says he was

An ancient statue of Ishtar, on display in a Syrian museum, brings to life the tale of the goddess of love, war, and fertility who commits cruel acts against those she loves, including turning a shepherd into a wolf.

walking with a soldier one night on his way to visit a lady friend. The moon was shining as bright as daylight. After the two men entered a cemetery, the soldier stripped off his clothing, turned into a wolf, and ran off howling into the woods. When Niceros tried to pick up the pile of clothing, he found it had turned to stone. Niceros said he was terrified: "No one could be nearer dead with terror than I was. But I drew my sword and went slaying shadows all the way till I came to my love's house. I went in—a mere ghost and nearly bubbled out my life; the sweat ran down my legs, my eyes were dull, I could hardly be revived."[5]

Niceros goes on to say that his story is absolutely true and that he would not make up such a horrible tale for any amount of money, calling on the angels to strike him down if he is lying. Later, Niceros was informed by his lady friend that after the soldier was transformed, a wolf attacked some sheep. It was driven off, however, when the shepherd stabbed the wolf in the neck. The following morning, Niceros went to the soldier's home and found the man in bed, suffering from a neck wound. In her book *Metamorphoses of the Werewolf*, Leslie A. Sconduto, professor of French at Bradley University in Illinois, explains the significance of this event: "This injury, which shows continuity between the bestial and human life and permits the identification of the werewolf, is an important motif in folklore. Even though Niceros had actually seen the soldier transform himself into a wolf, it is only when he finds the soldier in bed being treated by a doctor for his neck wound that he is convinced."[6]

Satyricon was a popular book, and Niceros's purported eyewitness account helped convince the public that humans could indeed be transformed into werewolves. The Roman scholar and writer Pliny the Elder attempted to persuade people otherwise. He wrote that werewolves were not real and that Niceros's account was untrue: "We are bound to pronounce with confidence that the story of men being turned into wolves and restored to themselves again is false—or else we must believe all the tales that the experience of so many centuries has taught us to be fabulous [fantasy]."[7]

Despite Pliny's efforts, the mythical beasts continued to be

Did You Know?

One of the earliest references to werewolves was written in ancient Mesopotamia more than 4,000 years ago.

associated with soldiers and the supernatural. In tenth-century Norway some of the most fearsome warriors were called the Úlfhednar or "wolf coated." It was believed that by dressing in wolf hides, the fighters, also called berserkers because of their berserk, or frenzied, behavior, were able to assume the spirits of wolves. This made each one stronger than seven men and gave them fearsome animal-like powers in battle. Writing in 1865, the English author and folklorist Sabine Baring-Gould described the frightening wolfish attributes of the Norse warriors:

> The berserkers were said to work themselves up to a state of frenzy, in which a demonical power came over them. . . . They acquired superhuman force, and were . . . invulnerable and . . . insensible to pain. No sword would wound them, no fire would burn them, a club alone could not destroy them, by breaking their bones or crushing their skulls. Their eyes glared as though a flame burned in the sockets, they ground their teeth, and frothed at the mouth; they gnawed at their shield rims, and are said to have sometimes bitten them through, and as they rushed into conflict they yelped as dogs or howled as wolves.[8]

Witches and Werewolves

The leader of the Úlfhednar, King Harald of Norway, was himself said to have had the body of a wolf and the head of a man. He was widely revered for this trait. However, as Christianity advanced across Europe during the Middle Ages, religious leaders began associating werewolves with heretical pagan beliefs. The church taught that were-creatures were pure evil and directly linked to witchcraft, magic, and the devil. This led to the widespread slaughter of innocent men accused of werewolfism and women accused of witchcraft.

The witch panic began in 1486 when two Dominican friars, Heinrich Krämer and Jakob Sprenger, wrote a comprehensive manual called *Malleus Maleficarum*, or *The Witch's Hammer*. The book was allegedly sanctioned by Pope Innocent VIII. The pope's orders to seek out and destroy witches were printed in the introduction to the book.

The Witch's Hammer uses logic, debate, and examples to prove the proposition that witchcraft is real and that witches work in league with the devil. The book discloses the methods witches use to curse and bewitch others. It also describes witches as shape changers who can transform themselves and others into various animals.

Lycanthropy is discussed in a section of *The Witch's Hammer* called "Wolves which sometimes Seize and Eat Men and Children out of their Cradles; whether this also is a Glamour [spell] caused by Witches." Krämer writes, "There is incidentally a question concerning wolves, which sometimes snatch men and children out of their houses and eat them, and run about with such astuteness that by no skill or strength can they be hurt or captured."[9] The author concludes that these creatures are not true wolves but men who have been transformed into child-eating werewolves by witches.

The Witch's Hammer contains a quarter-million words and was reprinted in 14 editions between 1486 and 1521. The book is credited with creating a widespread acceptance among the European public of a direct link between Satan, witches, and

werewolves. Commenting on the influence of *The Witch's Hammer*, Sconduto writes, "In addition to affecting attitudes regarding witchcraft, the text shaped opinion about werewolves, for the belief in witches and their ability to transform themselves [and others] into animals also made the belief in werewolves permissible."[10] This resulted in at least 100,000 innocent people being arrested, tortured, and burned at the stake before the panic ended in the mid-1700s. While 80 percent of the victims were women charged with witchcraft, about 20,000 were men, most accused of werewolfism.

The success of *The Witch's Hammer* inspired dozens of others to write texts documenting the heinous deeds of witches, magicians, and werewolves. In 1658 Bishop Olaus Magnus wrote that werewolves were particularly troublesome in Prussia, Latvia, and Lithuania. Magnus said people suffered considerably from the creatures, which were even more vicious than the indigenous gray wolves. Magnus writes of vicious werewolf attacks on villagers:

> A multitude of wolves transformed from men . . . rage with wondrous ferocity against human beings. . . . When a human habitation has been detected by them isolated in the woods, they besiege it with atrocity, striving to break the doors, and in the event of their doing so, they devour all the human beings and . . . they burst into the beer cellars, and there they empty the [barrels] of beer or mead [wine], and pile up the casks one above the other in the middle of the cellar, thus showing their difference from natural and genuine wolves.[11]

Werewolves and Vampires

The werewolves of Serbia, Bulgaria, Romania, Russia, and Poland are often compared to vampires because of their shape-shifting powers and their taste for living flesh. In Serbia werewolves and vampires were once known as a single creature, the *vukolak*, meaning "wolf haired" or "wolf skinned." These beasts are werewolves when they are alive but become vampires after death. And once the creature becomes a vampire, it has the power to shape-shift back into a werewolf. Unlike vampires, which only stalk their victims at night, the *vukolak* can be seen hunting at any time. As Catholic theologian Leone Allacci wrote in 1645:

> [The *vukolak*] is said to be so fearfully destructive to men that it actually makes its appearance in the daytime, even at high noon, nor does it then confine its visits to houses, but even in the fields and in hedged vineyards and upon the open highway it will suddenly advance upon persons who are laboring, or travelers as they walk along, and by the horror of its hideous aspect it will slay them without laying hold on them or even speaking a word.[12]

In Romania the mountains and forests of the Transylvania region provide a home for the werewolf-vampire called a *vircolac*. Stories of this creature date back to ancient times, when wild wolves could be seen digging in cemeteries. The hungry wolves scavenged in burial grounds because corpses were buried in shallow graves and wrapped only in cloth shrouds. These decomposing remains produced gases that occasionally forced the bodies up to the surface. In addition to creating myths about the dead

rising from graves, this gruesome occurrence made cemeteries prime feeding grounds for wolves that would eat the fresh corpses. In *The Beast Within*, journalist Adam Douglas describes how these conditions led to the intermingling of vampire and werewolf lore:

> These real wolves, scavenging for grisly tidbits in burial grounds at night, could easily be misinterpreted by local observers as werewolves. . . . But the confusion between vampire and werewolf . . . suggests the possibility that someone seeing a real wolf attempting to dig up a human corpse and then making off into the night, might conclude that the corpse was that of a vampire, which then transferred its spirit into a werewolf, risen from the grave, and run away to cause mischief elsewhere.[13]

Born with a Caul

Whatever the basis for the mythology, belief in werewolves is deeply embedded in eastern European culture. As far back as the twelfth century, legends were told about Vseslav, who was called the werewolf prince of Polotsk, Belarus. Vseslav was born with a caul covering his face. A caul is a portion of the amniotic sac that clings to an infant as it is being born. It is considered good luck in many cultures. But in eastern Europe, caul bearers were seen as future werewolves or vampires. Prince Vseslav did not disappoint on this account. When he was only one hour old, he purportedly yelled out that he wanted a suit of armor instead of the soft cloth known as swaddling clothes. At the age of 12 Vseslav mastered the ability to transform himself into a werewolf. At age

An illustration depicts hungry wolves lined up outside a cemetery, waiting for the right moment to enter. The wolves were said to scratch up graves and gnaw on the bones of the corpses.

15, in the form of a werewolf, the prince led a bloody military campaign against Kiev (now the capital city of Ukraine). According to the twelfth-century epic poem *The Tale of Igor's Campaign*:

> Vseslav . . . vaulted toward the city of Kiev. . . . Like a fierce beast he leapt away from [his enemies] at midnight, out of the white town, having enveloped himself in a blue mist. Then at morn, he . . . loped like a wolf to the Nemiga [River]. . . . Vseslav the prince judged men; as prince, he ruled towns; but at night he prowled in the guise of a wolf.[14]

Variations on the story of Vseslav developed over time. In western Siberia the legend of Vseslav was transformed into the story of Volx, a magician who had traits of both werewolves and vampires. In the 1870s an anonymous poem describes Volx. He was the son of a prince, but his mother was a serpent. Born with a caul, the supernatural powers of Volx were exhibited at an early age, and his willingness to shed blood made Mother Earth herself tremble. According to the poem:

> [Volx] is omnipresent, exceedingly crafty, and wonderworking; the huntsman's luck accompanies his predacious venturesome quest for power over the animal and human kingdom. In vain his prospective victims strive to escape. Intimately allied with the

forces of night, he threatens the sun itself. Where he comes running in wolf-shape, there the earth becomes stained with blood, and vampiric ghosts hover over his abode. Glory and suffering are inseparably intertwined in the course of his life as a werewolf—hunter and [vampire].[15]

"A Compassionate Response"

Not all eastern Europeans believed in the evil nature of werewolves. The Romani people, commonly known as gypsies, believed that white wolves visited cemeteries to guard against vampires rising from graves. Gypsies also believed that werewolves would attack and kill vampires found wandering the countryside in search of human blood. This sympathetic view is based on the belief that werewolves themselves were victims. They were transformed from human to wolf as a form of punishment because their parents had broken religious taboos. Because they suffered for their parents' sins, werewolves were looked upon with empathy.

That is not to say that werewolves did not cause fear or anxiety among the Romani. Anyone who was attacked by such a creature had the right to use self-defense. But someone who deliberately murdered a werewolf would be punished with bad luck that might lead to death. Conversely, those who helped a werewolf might receive monetary rewards, as folklore expert Harry A. Senn explains in *Were-Wolf and Vampire in Romania:*

> [A] were-wolf may evoke a compassionate response from a worker or campers in the forest. In one popular legend, a wolf emerges from the woods and paces on the far side of a camp fire where food is cooking. The camper shares his

Among the Navajo of the Southwest, the term *skinwalker* is commonly used to describe evil witches who turn into werewolves.

slanina (pork fat) or bread with the hungry animal that finishes the food and departs. Later in a nearby village, the worker's wares are wholly purchased and he is richly rewarded by a wealthy landowner who confides that he, a were-wolf, had visited the man's camp as a wolf.[16]

Navajo Skinwalkers

The belief in shape-shifting werewolves is deeply rooted in other cultures, including those of India, China, Japan, and North America. Native Americans have long told stories about witches who become coyotes, owls, crows, and wolves.

Among the Navajo of the Southwest, the term *skinwalker* is commonly used to describe evil witches who turn into werewolves. The witches are called *yee naaldlooshii*, which translates to "with the skin, he goes on all fours" in the Navajo language. To become a skinwalker, witches don the skin of a wolf during a magic ceremony, which gives them the powers of a human wolf. In 1936 anthropologist William Morgan interviewed a Navajo man named Hajogo who described the characteristics of the skinwalker. Morgan's questions and comments are in parentheses:

> [Some] older men put on skins at night, a wolf skin . . . and they go around. They might kill a man. (Are they witches?) Yes. And they say they meet together, a man from way over there (east) meets a man from way over there (north), and they can go very fast. (How fast?) They can go to (Albuquerque) in an hour and a half. (It takes four hours by automobile.) And these men know how to make you sick.

The Gray Wolf

Fear of the werewolf reflects humanity's traditional attitudes toward the gray wolf, an ancestor of the domesticated dog. The gray wolf once roamed freely through the forests, deserts, grasslands, and mountains of North America, Europe, and Asia. However, it has been hunted to extinction or near extinction almost everywhere. While some cultures respect and revere the wolf, others have tried to eliminate it because at times it preys on sheep, goats, and other livestock. In addition, there is an unfounded belief that wolves will attack and kill humans. While there have been reports of such behavior over the centuries, wolves that bite people are usually found to be suffering from rabies, a viral disease that makes them extremely aggressive. Rabid wolves will bite nearly any living creature. However, healthy wolves are usually timid around humans, and nonrabid wolf attacks are extremely rare. Despite the animals' generally passive behavior toward humans, the ancient fear and hatred of werewolves can be traced to centuries of human interaction with the gray wolf.

. . . (What kind of tracks would one of those men make?) They would be big, like a big paw.[17]

Skinwalkers commit their evil deeds by stunning their victims with a noxious powder. This pollen-like substance, called bad medicine, is purportedly made from the dried flesh and ground-up bones of dead people. The most potent powder is made from the necks, fingertips, and tongues of strong men, pretty young girls, and children, especially twins.

The death dust is often administered to sleeping victims. Navajos traditionally lived in hogans, round houses made of logs and earth. Skinwalkers are said to climb on the roofs of hogans and drop powder down the smoke hole at the center of the structure. According to a Navajo elder named Kejoji:

> [The powder is] like matches. It makes the fire blaze up for just a second and then they can see where the person is that they want to kill. They have poison on a stick or on a stone and they put that in front of the person's face. And when they breathe it they die. . . . The spirit of the dead person [whose body parts are in the powder] would come after them and kill them.[18]

The substance can also be slipped into a cigarette, drink, or serving of food. When ingested, the bad medicine can cause a variety of ailments before the victim dies. These include a black and swollen tongue, unconsciousness, flulike symptoms, tuberculosis, or tetanus, which causes severe muscle spasms and stiffness.

The Navajo have many stories about skinwalkers that are exposed, hunted, and killed. The creatures are often discovered when they make noises or knock dirt down after climbing up on a hogan roof. This alerts inhabitants, who run outside to wound the creature with a gun, knife, or ax. In such stories the skinwalker usually runs off but is tracked down by someone following its large paw prints or the trail of blood from its injury. Invariably, the tracks lead to a dying person who claims he or she was wounded by accident. But it is somehow revealed that the person is really a skinwalker and the injury occurred when he or she was in the guise of a human wolf. Hajogo's wife Yadiba related a typical werewolf tale that she said took place when she was a little girl. The story begins after a 15-year-old boy sees some dirt fall from the ceiling of the hogan where he lived with his two younger sisters:

> And he took his gun and he went outside; it was snowing. That is when those human-wolves like to come out because the snow covers up their tracks. . . . The wolf ran behind some trees, but the lad went out and shot him in the side. Then in the morning he took [his two sisters] and they followed his tracks. They could see because the blood leaves a yellow mark. They followed about twelve miles . . . and he found a place where the human-wolf had lain down and there was lots of blood and some rags. He thinks he used the rags to wipe off the blood. [The werewolf] must have taken off the skin there because he could find no more tracks. Two days later he heard a man died (about thirty miles away). It was said he had fallen off his horse and hurt his side. But [the boy] thinks that was the

man he shot; but he didn't say anything, and he didn't even tell the girls he shot a human-wolf.[19]

Werewolf of the Swamps

Werewolf stories are common in other parts of the United States, in particular in Louisiana. When French Cajuns first settled there in the 1760s, people spoke of a beast that lived in the swamps around New Orleans. The creature was called a *rougarou*, a term similar to *loup-garou*, the French word for werewolf.

The rougarou is described as having a human body and the head of a wolf. Anyone bitten by the creature transforms into a rougarou for 101 days. During that time, the victim is a pale, sick person by day. At night, however, the rougarou regains its vitality, leaves its bed, and scurries through the countryside in search of victims to bite. By attacking a victim the beast can break the spell and pass the rougarou curse on to someone else.

With so many stories in so many different places, the dread of werewolves would seem to be universal. Psychologists say this fear is not based in reality but can be traced to anxieties that reside deep in the human subconscious. People have deep-seated fears of cannibalism, animal transformation, and creatures that wander through the night, and these fears surface at times in the form of terrifying stories. Those who claim to have encountered werewolves know that their stories sound incredible, yet they do not doubt the reality of their experiences. They warn that those who disregard such claims as nonsense may be fools.

Do werewolves truly exist? Or are they phantoms born of fear and overactive minds? Whichever the case, from ancient Mesopotamia to the local movie theater, werewolves have succeeded in making their beastly mark on human culture and history.

Opposite: Werewolves are known as loup-garou *in parts of the French-speaking world. An engraving depicts a French Canadian* loup-garou *legend. French-speaking Cajuns in Louisiana believed that werewolves, which they called* rougarou, *lurked in the swamps.*

CHAPTER 2

From Human to Wolf

For many centuries people's lives were intimately intertwined with wolves. Hunters donned complete wolf skins that included heads with sharp, snarling fangs exposed. The skins transformed the hunters into wolf men who could fiercely stalk the same prey pursued by wolves, including deer, elk, bison, and wild pigs. The hunters sometimes even shared their shelters with wolves, inhabiting the same caves and crevices in the rocks. Then, using magical rituals revealed to shamans during dreams, visions, hallucinations, and prophecy, some hunters tried to shape-shift into werewolves to complete the transformation.

"Make Me a Man-Eater!"

In 1912 Irish psychic investigator Elliot O'Donnell described ancient magic rituals people used for centuries in Russia and Siberia to change, or metamorphose, into wolves. In *Werewolf* O'Donnell says that supplicants, or those wishing to perform werewolf magic, traveled deep into the dark forest because the "powers to be petitioned are not found . . . anywhere. They favor only such wastes and solitary places as the deserts, woods, and mountaintops."[20] The phase of the moon also seems to have played a role in such rituals. O'Donnell wrote that the ritual must be conducted during a new moon. At this time the night is darkest and "superphysical presences are much in evidence on earth."[21] Others say werewolf transformation ceremonies required a full moon. As British author Ian Woodward explains in *The Werewolf Delusion*, "At this time the earth is literally 'bathed' in sinister supernatural presences."[22] A third option is described in ancient books of magic that say transformation spells are best undertaken whenever the moon is growing larger, or waxing.

But perhaps the attitude of the petitioner is most important. He or she must truly believe in the mystical powers of the spell about to be performed. The supplicant begins by making two circles on the ground, one larger than the other, using chalk, string, or powdered coal. A fire is kindled in the inner circle using wood from the black poplar, pine, or larch. Once the fire is bright, the petitioner must place an iron pot in the center of the fire and cast into it a magical herb mixture that has been previously prepared. The concoction consists of several common herbs such as parsley and poppy seed, but it also contains toxic substances like henbane, hemlock, and the powerful addictive drug opium.

A magical spell is then recited. The words to one such spell are provided by Woodward:

> Make me a werewolf strong and bold,
> The terror alike of young and old,
> Grant me a figure tall and spare;
> The speed of the elk, the claws of the bear;
> The poison of snakes, the wit of the fox;
> The stealth of the wolf, the strength of the ox;
> The jaws of the tiger, the teeth of the shark;
> The eyes of a cat that sees in the dark.
> Make me climb like a monkey, scent like a dog,
> Swim like a fish, and act like a hog. . . .
> When I die I will serve thee evermore,
> Evermore in gray wolf land, cold and raw.[23]

The words are meant to put the supplicant in an agitated state. During this part of the ceremony, it is necessary to kiss the ground three times. The supplicant then grabs the iron pot off the fire and whirls the smoking cauldron around his or her head. More words are recited as the supplicant impels the spirits: "Make me a werewolf! Make me a man-eater! . . . Great Wolf Spirit! Give it to me, and . . . I am yours."[24]

Calling on the Great Wolf Spirit

As the spell is cast, the supplicant strips off his or her clothes and smears his or her body with a witch's ointment made of animal fat mixed with belladonna, henbane, and other herbs. Scientists say that the potent herbs used in such ointments are absorbed by the skin and can cause hallucinations and odd behavior.

Opposite: Native Americans of the Great Plains don wolf skins while hunting bison. By covering themselves in wolf skins, hunters hoped to take on the hunting prowess and stealth of this much-admired creature.

Belladonna, for example, causes laughter, restlessness, talkativeness, and disturbing visions. Henbane contains potent alkaloids that cause temporary insanity. This prompted William Shakespeare to describe henbane as "the insane root that takes reason prisoner."[25]

As the effects of the witch's ointment take hold, the supplicant places a belt made of wolf skin, called a wolf strap, around his or her waist. At this time, the Great Wolf Spirit, also called the Unknown, arrives. The scene is described by an unnamed witness quoted by Woodward:

> [Trees] begin to rustle, and the wind to moan, and out of the sudden darkness that envelops everything glowed the tall, cylindrical, pillar-like phantom of the Unknown, seven or eight feet in height. It sometimes developed further and assumed the form of a tall, thin monstrosity, half human and half animal, grey and nude, with very long legs and arms, and the feet and claws of a wolf. Its head was shaped like that of a wolf, but surrounded with the hair of a woman, that fell about its bare shoulders in yellow ringlets. It had wolf's ears, and a wolf's mouth. Its aquiline nose and pale eyes were fashioned like those of a human being, but animated with an expression too diabolically malignant to proceed from anything but the [supernatural]. It seldom spoke, but either uttered some extraordinary noise—a prolonged howl that seemed to proceed from the bowels of the earth, a piercing, harrowing whine, or a low laugh full of hellish glee. . . . It only remained visible for a minute at the most, and then disappeared with startling abruptness.[26]

Opposite: Spells and rituals for transforming humans into wolves depend on the phases of the moon (pictured). Some rituals require a new moon while others work best as the moon grows larger.

Many have speculated on the nature of this phantasm. Some say the Great Wolf Spirit is just one of many devilish spirits that haunt the deep woods. However, those who studied demons during the Middle Ages, called demonologists, believed that the transformational spirit was Satan himself, the embodiment of all evil.

Whatever the true identity of the Great Wolf Spirit, when it appears the temperature suddenly drops, and the sounds of crashing, banging, groaning, and howling ring out. The spirit then presents the supplicant with the "gift of lycanthropy,"[27] O'Donnell writes. The next evening at sunset, the petitioner becomes a ravening werewolf. The following dawn, he or she returns to human form. This cycle continues every passing night until the werewolf's death. If the supplicant dies while in human form, he or

One werewolf spell seeks to combine the strengths of many animals into one. It calls for the speed of an elk, the claws of a bear (pictured), the poison of snakes, the wit of a fox, the stealth of a wolf, the strength of an ox, and more.

she transforms one final time into a werewolf while gasping for a last breath. However, if the supplicant dies in werewolf form, he or she transforms back to human form upon death.

The Wolf Strap

The magical talisman called a wolf strap or wolf belt plays an important role in almost all werewolf transformations. In 1925 German author Adolph Wuttke described the wolf strap in *The German People and Superstition of the Present:*

> People (men, women, even boys) change, mostly just for several hours, into wolves by wearing a wolf belt on the naked body (sometimes also on clothes). [This belt is made of] wolf's leather [and sometimes] human skin, especially the skin of a hanged man, often adorned with the zodiac, and with seven tongues on the buckle [which must be put] into the ninth hole; if they want to return to their human form, they open the buckle.[28]

Once a person straps on a wolf belt, he or she will purportedly undergo profound physical and mental transformations. Whether man, woman, or child, the werewolf will produce one long bushy eyebrow that stretches across the forehead from ear to ear. The ears themselves become pointed and move back and lower on the head. The teeth turn red and grow long and sharp, with the cuspids, or canine teeth, extending into fangs. The third finger also lengthens, the fingernails turn into razor-sharp talons, and hair grows on the palms. It is said that werewolves have dry mouths and they are thirsty, presumably for blood, at all times. The eyes

are also dry. And according to demonologists, werewolves, like witches, cannot weep.

Werewolf flesh is often covered with scabs since the creatures are scratched as they run through brush and bramble. Battle scars are evident from fighting with wild animals and human attackers. The skin that is not covered with rough fur is yellow or greenish. When the creature moves about, it either lopes silently on two legs or moves about on all fours, with a supernatural ability to leap long distances to gain on its prey. Oftentimes, the creature's buttocks are branded with a symbol called the devil's mark.

The emotional state of werewolves has been described most often as depressed and downhearted. Having made a pact with the devil, they feel that their fate is inescapable. As Montague Summers, an investigator of the supernatural, writes, "By very force of his evil pact with hell he cannot in any whit [free] himself from the shedding of blood and bestial savagery."[29] The melancholy is multiplied because werewolves retain the ability to think and reason like humans but are unable to speak or communicate, except by howling and growling. And once the wolf mind mingles with the human brain, other personality traits become painfully obvious. Werewolves, even in their human form during the day, exhibit symptoms such as aggression, violent behavior, unprovoked rages, insomnia, and restlessness.

In League with the Devil

During the early nineteenth century in southern France, it was commonly believed that the illegitimate sons of priests were compelled to become werewolves. This was particularly true in the district of Périgord, where it was said that such young men went forth during the full moon and plunged naked into a certain lake. When they emerged, they found wolf straps left for them by the devil. After putting on the belts, the transformed boys traveled in packs wreaking havoc on the countryside until dawn. As the sun rose over the hills, the wolf boys took off the belts, jumped back into the lake, and emerged as normal teenagers.

A popular story told in this region begins with a group of teenage girls tending sheep in the hills around Périgord. The girls come upon a 13-year-old boy who has a strange appearance. His hair is tawny red and falls in thick mats over his shoulders and narrow forehead. He has small, wild eyes, gray in color, that are sunken deeply in his head. His teeth look like fangs, and his hands are large, with long, sharp nails. His clothes are in tatters and hang off his body.

The boy appears to be starving, so the girls take pity on him and begin to talk to him. The boy tells them his name is Jean and he is the son of a priest. Jean says he puts on a wolf strap the hour before sunset three days a week. This changes him into a werewolf, and he runs about the countryside with a pack of nine others just like him. Jean says he sold his soul to the devil in exchange for the wolf strap. He says that while wearing the wolf strap, he prefers to eat pretty girls like those standing before him. He goes on to describe the victims he has already eaten. The girls run away after hearing this story, but report Jean to police because several young women have recently disappeared from the village.

The story of the wolf boy Jean ends there, but similar tales have been told in villages throughout Europe for centuries. According to Summers, during a sixteenth-century French werewolf trial, two men accused of lycanthropy told a judge that "Satan clothed them in a wolf's skin which completely covered them, and . . .

In the magical transformation from human to werewolf, the ears, teeth, and fingernails experience dramatic changes. The teeth grow long and sharp until they resemble the teeth and jaws of a wolf (pictured).

they then went about on all-fours and ran around the country chasing now a person and now an animal according to the guidance of their appetites."[30]

Some took pity on those who possessed wolf belts because the straps were purportedly impossible to destroy. In 1898 two folklore researchers, Ferdinand Asmus and Otto Knoop, described problems with a wolf belt in Germany:

> About sixty years ago in Alt-Marrin there lived a man by the name of [Gustav] K. He too possessed a wolf strap, with which he brought about much damage and misery. Finally the strap was taken from him, and it was to be burned. Three times the baking oven was heated up, and three times the

strap was thrown into the glowing fire, but each time it jumped back out of the flames. Nor would water damage the strap. It always returned.[31]

Wolf Waters

There are alternative methods to becoming a werewolf that do not involve wolf straps. In Norway and Sweden it is believed a supplicant can achieve transformation by sipping rainwater from the footprint of a wolf at midnight. Alternatively, he or she may wait for a full moon night and find a stream where three or more wolves have been observed quenching their thirst. Upon finding this location the petitioner must chant a spell that ends with the words:

> Oh water strong, that swirls along,
> I prithee [pray thee] a werewolf make me.
> Of all things dear, my soul, I swear,
> In death shall not forsake thee.[32]

The incantation is followed by an oath sworn to the Phantom of Darkness, during which the supplicant strikes his or her forehead on the riverbank three times. The supplicant then thrice submerges his or her head in the stream and gulps mouthfuls of the water. Twenty-four hours later he or she will become a werewolf.

The magical liquid found in flowing streams where wolves drink is called lycanthropous water, described by O'Donnell:

> A strange, faint odor, comparable with nothing, distinguishes lycanthropous water; there is a lurid sparkle in it, strongly suggestive of some peculiar, individual life; the noise it makes, as it rushes along,

Mistaken
for Werewolves

By most measures, Danny Ramos Gomez is a regular kind of guy. He is in his 20s and has a girlfriend. He likes to play football and video games and go to the movies. But in one major way Gomez is not like other men his age. He is covered with thick hair. He has so much hair on his face and body that his girlfriend has never actually seen his face.

Gomez has an extremely rare genetic disorder called hypertrichosis. Hypertrichosis causes people to grow

so closely resembles the muttering and whispering of human voices as to be often mistaken for them; whilst at night it sometimes utters piercing screams, and howls, and groans, in such a manner as to terrify all who pass near it. Dogs and horses, in particular, are susceptible to its influence, and they exhibit the greatest signs of terror at the mere sound of it.[33]

thick hair, up to 10 inches long, all over their faces and bodies. Researchers believe that at least some of the people described as werewolves throughout history might have suffered from this disorder.

In 2007 the television show *Primetime* featured Gomez and other members of his family. Although the disease only affects about 1 out of every 100 million people, 20 people in the Gomez family have hypertrichosis. Gomez told *Primetime* he is not affected by the way he looks. "I am the same as everybody, except what you see on my face, that's all."

Quoted in John Quiñones, Laura Viddy, and Cecile Bouchardeau, "Real-Life 'Were-wolves,'" *ABC Primetime*, September 12, 2007. http://abcnews.go.com.

The plants growing around magical streams are also said to possess transformative powers. Long ago, Swedish and Norwegian peasants who wished to become werewolves plucked lycanthropous flowers after sunset. These were worn in the hair or on the clothing by supplicants. While the blossoms looked like normal white or yellow flowers, they possessed a faint scent of death and oozed sap that is unpleasantly white and sticky.

Low Spirits and Evil Thoughts

Some unfortunate souls did not wish to become werewolves but were cursed with lycanthropy as a result of bad behavior. Being denounced by a priest from the pulpit was a sure way to become a werewolf. In Normandy, France, for example, it was long believed that any man who was excommunicated was in danger of becoming a werewolf for either three or seven years, depending on his offense. In nearby Basse-Bretange anyone who had not confessed his sins for a period of 10 years was also said to be a candidate for werewolfism.

People associated with crimes might also be threatened with lycanthropy. For example, a person might turn into a werewolf if he or she witnessed a crime but refused to testify against the criminal in court. And criminals who escaped punishment could also expect to suffer from werewolfism. This might explain why in centuries past the word for "wolf," *warg*, was used by court authorities in Germany to describe outlaws and robbers. A similar Old English term, *wearg*, describes a strangler and is also the word for "wolf."

How a criminal can turn into a werewolf may have a spiritual rather than earthly explanation. The answer concerns the state of the spirit or soul. Religious thinkers have written that certain criminals are so evil that their spirits are different from those of average citizens. These low spirits can mingle with animal spirits, transforming the outlaw into an animal. As Woodward explains:

> It is just possible for a man to live a life so absolutely depraved, so utterly wicked and brutal, that the whole of his lower mind may be enmeshed in his desires, and finally separated from . . . the higher

self. . . . These low forces . . . can be formed into or given the shape of, animals; these thought-forms can be energized . . . and directed on a mission of bloodshed.[34]

British psychic and occult researcher Rose Gladden, who died in 1985, worked with dozens of people who claimed to be possessed by werewolf spirits. It was Gladden's belief that people can direct their low spirits into images of werewolves. She worked with a 17-year-old boy named Tommy who claimed to use the powers of his lower spirit to punish his enemies.

Tommy hated people. As a child he wore thick glasses and was considered ugly, which left him open to merciless ridicule. Tommy found out, however, that he could make his tormenters sick. He did this by concentrating on them very strongly while wishing them bad luck and sickness. When he saw that his efforts were working, Tommy even began to wish death upon his enemies. Eventually, the boy claimed that his low, evil thoughts took the form of wolves. The wolves not only attacked his enemies, but bounced back to attack Tommy himself. Gladden picks up the story:

> It means he was being attacked by the manifestation of his own evil thoughts. They were in the form of . . . wolves. And do remember that when his enemies were . . . [attacked], that what they caught sight of on each occasion was a savage [werewolf]—a savage animal coming at *them.* That animal, that wolf, would have been very real to them. . . . It could have [seemed real] to the point of having them sent to a mental hospital. [35]

"People (men, women, even boys) change, mostly just for several hours, into wolves by wearing a wolf belt on the naked body."

—German author Adolph Wuttke describing the power of the wolf strap.

Werewolf Children

Whether evil thoughts or low spirits can manifest themselves as bloodthirsty werewolves is uncertain. But some have put forth another explanation for werewolfism. Since the 1600s there have been numerous reports of feral children, also known as wolf children. These are children who were raised by wolves and who had minimal contact with humans. In almost all cases the children were found naked, could not talk, and walked on all fours with calloused hands. The wolf children ate raw food and had animal characteristics that included barking, biting, and snarling at those who tried to help them.

There have been over 100 cases of children raised by wolves. The earliest cases date to fourteenth-century Germany and the most recent was documented in the early 1970s in India. In the eighteenth century alone, so many cases of wolf children were reported that Swedish scientist Carl von Linné classified them as a separate species, *Homo ferus*, or feral man. It was commonly believed that although these wolf children were born to human parents, they were carried into the forest by wolves as babies.

One of the most astonishing cases of wolf children concerns two girls discovered to be living with wolves in the Indian state of Orissa. The girls were discovered by a Christian missionary, the Reverend J.A.L. Singh, in the Bengal jungle in October 1920. Singh was visiting a region inhabited by indigenous people called the Santals, when he was told of ghosts who lived in the nearby jungle. The ghosts were described as man-beasts—humans with ferocious animal heads. Singh believed the story was superstitious nonsense but decided to investigate, visiting the area where the beasts were said to live. He found a gigantic anthill that had been abandoned by the insects. Wolves had moved in, hollowing out the base to make a den for their pups.

Singh watched the anthill for hours at a time and recorded the wolves coming and going. However, at one point he was startled to see that two of the wild animals were not wolves. According to Singh's diary, the first creature he saw was

> a hideous-looking being—hand, foot, and body like a human being; but the head was a big ball of something covering the shoulders and the upper portion of the bust, leaving only a sharp contour of the face visible, and it was human. Close at its heels there came another awful creature exactly like the first, but smaller in size. Their eyes were bright and piercing, unlike human eyes. I at once came to the conclusion that these were human beings.[36]

Singh rounded up a crew of local villagers and had them cut a hole in the anthill. As they were doing so, several wolves ran out, including a she-wolf that seemed to be nurturing the creatures inside. The female wolf put up a terrible fight but was killed, leaving Singh and his assistants to take the top off the mound. Inside, two wolf girls were curled up in a tight, protective ball with two wolf cubs. When Singh tried to rescue them, the girls fought ferociously, biting and scratching like wild animals. Finally, they were captured and taken to an orphanage. Singh named the feral children Kamala, Bengali for "lotus," and Amala, or "bright yellow flower."

Even after Kamala and Amala were cleaned up and given haircuts, they continued to act like wolves. They refused to stand upright and seemed unable to straighten their limbs when lifted. They could run as fast as a squirrel on all fours but often sat in the corner of a room, aloof and unaware of human activities around them. However, their senses were much more acute than those of normal humans, according to Singh:

> They had a powerful instinct and could smell meat or anything from a great distance like animals. . . . Kamala smelled meat from a distance of seventy yards and ran quickly to the kitchen veranda, where meat was being dressed. With a ferocious look, she tried to grab it, her eyes rolling, jaws moving from side to side, and teeth chattering while she made a fearful growling sound, neither human or animal.[37]

On another occasion Kamala was seen feasting on the bloody carcass of a dead cow that was surrounded by vultures. And Amala purportedly wrestled a bone away from an orphanage dog and took it to the corner, where she ravenously chewed on it like a wild beast. At night the children prowled the orphanage howling like wolves. Sometimes the wolf girls viciously attacked other children but rarely caused lasting harm because they were under close supervision.

Kamala and Amala lived at the orphanage while Singh kept a detailed diary of their activities. The entire time, they ate, lived, slept, and even relieved themselves like wild wolves. Amala did not live very long in captivity, dying on September 21, 1921 from a kidney infection. In the years that followed, Kamala began to change. She learned to walk upright, eat regular food, and speak

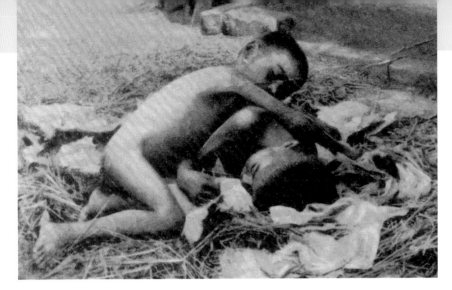

Kamala and Amala, two feral children found to be living with wolves in India in 1920, sleep more like wolf cubs than human children in this photograph. The two girls were captured and taken to an orphanage where they were taught human behaviors.

a few words. However, Kamala died in 1929, when she was about 16 years old, leaving Singh to conclude: "Untimely death cut short the fascinating study of the tardy development of this human being from a wolflike existence to that of a human being."[38]

In the 1970s investigator Charles Maclean conducted an exhaustive inquiry concerning the wolf girls of Orissa. After interviewing witnesses and studying photos of the girls, Maclean concluded that they were truly raised by wolves and that Singh's diary and observations were accurate. This might help to explain other werewolf sightings reported over the centuries. If these two girls truly lived as wolves, others might have shared the same fate—leaving a trail of blood across the countryside. Then again, such carnage could also have resulted from evil or mentally disturbed individuals who claimed werewolf possession to justify their heinous crimes. Or it just might be possible that werewolves really exist and magic spells and moonlight can transform a regular person into a ravaging beast.

CHAPTER 3

Werewolves on the Prowl

In November 1987 Fox Broadcasting Company began airing a Saturday-night mystery series called *Werewolf*. Fox had been on the air for little more than a year, and *Werewolf* was languishing near the bottom of the viewer ratings. In order to attract attention to the network and promote the show, Fox set up a Werewolf Hotline. When each episode of *Werewolf* concluded, an announcer asked people to call the hotline to find out more about werewolves. After the first week Fox received over 340,000 telephone calls, along with 500 letters sent to company headquarters. Some viewers said they had encountered werewolves, and others blamed unsolved murders in their town on werewolves. A small minority even claimed that they themselves were werewolves. And four people mailed in what they said were werewolf hair specimens. These were turned over to California's state crime lab, but the scientific results were inconclusive.

After attracting so much attention with its Werewolf Hotline, Fox hired New York paranormal investigator Steven Kaplan to appear on network talk shows to discuss werewolves in America. According to Kaplan, "I decided to [participate] because people who believe they are werewolves have no one . . . to talk to without being called evil. Throughout the years we have interviewed 15 people whom I believe are werewolves, and I estimate that there are 225 to 250 in North America alone."[39]

"Abominable Crimes"

If Kaplan's numbers are correct, there was about 1 werewolf for every 1.25 million people living in North America in 1987. That statistic cannot compare to sixteenth-century France, when werewolves seemed to be living in nearly every city and town. Attacks were reported with horrific regularity, and court records from that time contain detailed accounts of rape, murder, and cannibalism blamed on werewolves. One of the most sensational cases concerned a social outcast who was tried in 1573 at the Supreme Court of the Parliament of Dole.

Dole is located in the heavily forested Franche-Comté region in the Jura mountain range of eastern France. Around 1571 there were several eyewitness reports in the region concerning children who were kidnapped by a werewolf. The populace was so alarmed that the parliament eventually stepped in and decreed that citizens should stockpile pikes, axes, javelins, firearms called arquebuses, and even clubs and wooden sticks. So armed, they could "chase and pursue the said werewolf in every place where they may find or seize him; to tie and to kill, without incurring any pains or penalties."[40]

"Throughout the years we have interviewed 15 people whom I believe are werewolves, and I estimate that there are 225 to 250 in North America alone."

—Paranormal investigator Steven Kaplan.

In September 1573, several months after the proclamation was issued, the vigilantes rescued a young girl from a wolf near La Poupée. The girl was bleeding from five deep bite wounds, and the rescuers believed the wolf had human features. Several villagers said they recognized the attacker and identified him as Gilles Garnier. Although he was married, Garnier was known as the Hermit of St. Bonnot. He and his wife lived in a small hut made from dirt and lichen-covered turf isolated in a deep forest glen. When he occasionally appeared in public, Garnier startled townsfolk with his crude appearance. His skin appeared bluish and bruised, and he carried a somber expression. The hermit had sunken eyes; coarse, bushy eyebrows that grew from ear to ear; wild, uncombed hair; and a long, unruly beard. He walked with a stooping gait and rarely spoke.

Six days after the first girl disappeared in La Poupée, another girl was reported missing. The Hermit of St. Bonnot was promptly arrested along with his wife, Apolline. In an indictment, read aloud in court, Garnier was accused of lycanthropy. Jean Bodin, the prosecuting lawyer, described Garnier's crimes in the 1580 book *On the Demon-Mania of Witches*:

> Garnier, on the day of Saint Michael [September 29], being in the form of a Were Wolf took a young girl ten or twelve years old near the woods of Serre, in a vineyard . . . and there he killed and butchered her, as much with his hands in the semblance of paws as with his teeth, and he ate the flesh of her thighs and arms, and he carried some to his wife. And [he took] another girl, and killed her in order

Opposite: Accounts of werewolf attacks were common in medieval France. In one region eyewitnesses reported kidnappings of children by werewolves, a scene depicted by this hand-colored woodcut.

to eat her, [but was] prevented by three people, as he has confessed. And fifteen days later, [Garnier] strangled a young child ten years old in the vineyard of Gredsans, and [ate] the flesh of his thighs, legs, and belly.[41]

Garnier, in human form, also killed a 12-year-old boy. This proved to be his undoing. He was discovered committing the crime and was recognized as the Hermit of St. Bonnot. Garnier was quickly convicted of being a werewolf, a child murderer, and a cannibal. He was burned at the stake, according to Bodin, "for the abominable crimes of lycanthropy and witchcraft,"[42] and his ashes were scattered in the wind.

"Horrible to Look Upon"

Garnier's execution proved to be a temporary solution to an ongoing problem in the Franche-Comté region. In fact, reports of werewolves only increased in the following decade. One of the most unusual cases concerned a 16-year-old boy, Benoit Bidel, who was in an apple orchard near the town of St. Claude with his younger sister in 1584. Bidel was in a tree picking fruit when a werewolf attacked his sister. The beast was very large and had a fur-covered face, no tail, and human hands. Bidel jumped down from the tree to defend his sister, but the werewolf killed him before nearby peasants could rush to his aid. The werewolf was pursued into the woods, where it was cornered and ripped apart by the crowd. However, the attackers were shocked when, upon death, the creature transformed back into human form and was recognized as a local woman named Perrenette Gandillon.

Soon after the apple orchard incident, Perrenette's sister Antoinette was arrested. While being tortured she admitted attending a witches' sabbat, or ceremony, where she claimed she made love to the devil. Afterward she metamorphosed into a werewolf and caused hail to destroy local crops. Perrenette's brother Pierre was also arrested, along with his son George. Both men were accused of witchcraft and lycanthropy. According to Henri Boguet, the lawyer who prosecuted them, the Gandillons

> were in the habit of anointing themselves with the Devil's unguent [ointment] and assuming the form and fierceness of wolves, under which shape they had murdered and eaten many young children. [They] were horrible to look upon, having lost well-nigh any resemblance to humanity, loping on all fours rather than walking upright, creatures with foul horny nails, unpared and sharp as talons, keen white teeth, matted hair, and gleaming red eyes.[43]

The entire Gandillon family was hanged and their corpses were burned to ashes. Yet attacks continued in the region. In 1598 a homeless beggar named Jacques Roulet admitted to eating a child after his hands, feet, face, and teeth turned into those of a wolf. That same year a tailor in Châlons was accused of lycanthropy after it was discovered he had been killing children in his shop. The Demon Tailor, as he was called, butchered his victims like farm animals and dissolved their bones in barrels of acid. Further details concerning the Demon Tailor were so shocking that all documents pertaining to the trial were destroyed by an order of the court.

*Opposite:
The torture
wheel brought
confessions
from accused
heretics during
the Spanish
Inquisition,
as depicted in
this engraving.
This method of
obtaining con-
fessions may
also explain the
large number
of convicted
werewolves
in medieval
France.*

It is unknown why lycanthropy appeared to be out of control in the Jura mountain region during this period. However, it is well known today that people will admit to almost anything while being tortured. There is little doubt that a person having limbs stretched on the rack or bones broken on the wheel would claim to be a werewolf if only to stop the pain.

Historians believe that not all cases of werewolfism from that era were based on public hysteria. The end of the sixteenth century was a difficult time in France. Excessive rain killed crops, and starvation and disease were rampant. It is entirely possible that the Demon Tailor and others were deranged from hunger and turned to cannibalism. Whatever, the case, records show that over 600 people were prosecuted for witchcraft and lycanthropy in the area between 1598 and 1616.

The Werewolf of Bedburg

Werewolf fears and gory murder trials were not confined to France. In neighboring Germany one of the most notorious cases in the annals of lycanthropy was reported in 1589. The criminal charges, torture, and execution of Peter Stubbe (also spelled Stump, Stumpf, or Stubb) were well known due to a lurid 16-page pamphlet published in several languages and sold throughout Europe in the years after his trial.

Stubbe was born in Bedburg, a small village near Cologne, around 1525, and by 1582 he was a prosperous farmer. But terror was stalking the countryside in the Bedburg region. Farmers began finding arms and legs of dead women and children scattered about in the fields and forests. While some believed this to be the grisly work of a ravenous wolf, the gruesome discoveries excited fears that a werewolf might be on the prowl. The carnage

continued for years, until one night in 1589 a group of farmers patrolling a rural area caught sight of a fearsome beast. Hunting dogs cornered the creature, and the citizens were amazed to see the horrible wolf shape-shift into their neighbor Peter Stubbe.

Stubbe was dragged off to prison and strapped onto the wheel. While suffering the excruciating pains of torture, Stubbe admitted that he had been inclined to evil since the age of 12, when he began practicing the wicked art of sorcery. By the time he was 20, Stubbe said he had given both his body and soul to the devil, who in return gave him a wolf belt. This transformed the German farmer into a greedy, devouring wolf with large eyes that sparkled like fire in the night. His body grew large, his hands transformed into huge paws, and his mouth filled with sharp, cruel teeth. According to the English pamphlet "The Damnable Life and Death of Stubbe Peeter," published in 1601, after becoming a werewolf:

> Stubbe Peeter herewith . . . proceeded to the execution of [various] most heinous and vile murders; for if any person displeased him, he would [exhibit an] incontinent thirst for revenge, and no sooner should they or any of theirs walk abroad in the fields or about the city, but in the shape of a wolf he would presently encounter them, and never rest till he had plucked out their throats and [torn] their joints asunder. . . . And sundry times he would go through the streets of Cologne [and] Bedburg . . . in comely habit, and very civilly, as one well known to all the inhabitants thereabout, and oftentimes was he saluted of those whose friends and children he had butchered, though nothing suspected for the same.[44]

A Savory and Delicious Meal

Stubbe's lycanthropic deeds allegedly took place over the course of 25 years. During this time the Werewolf of Bedburg, as he became known, also killed goats, lambs, and sheep. In addition, he devoured and ate large portions of 14 children, 2 men, and 2 pregnant women. But Stubbe's monstrous crimes did not end there. Although he had often been heard talking to neighbors about the love he held for his firstborn son, according to the pamphlet, "in the shape and likeness of a wolf he encountered his own son and there most cruelly slew him, which done, he presently ate the brains out of his head as a most savory and dainty delicious meal to staunch his greedy appetite: the most monstrous act that ever man heard of."[45]

Only the harshest punishments could satisfy the public's demand for revenge. The court record spelled out his sentence, which was carried out on October 31, 1589:

> Stubbe Peeter as principal malefactor, was judged first to have his body laid on a wheel, and with red hot burning pincers in ten. . . places to have the flesh pulled off from the bones, after that, his legs and arms to be broken with a wooden ax or hatchet, afterward to have his head struck from his body, then to have his carcass burned to ashes.[46]

Stubbe was not the only one punished for his sins. His daughter and mistress were judged accessories to his crimes. Both were strangled, and their bodies were burned.

The pamphlet detailing Stubbe's crimes reached far and wide. Many judged him to be a werewolf of the worst sort, although it

Brute Animals

At the end of the sixteenth century, the French were suffering from starvation and disease. Some researchers say this might explain why so many were arrested for lycanthropy and convicted of cannibalism. In *The Beast Within*, Adam Douglas explains:

> 1598 was another cold, wet year in a terrible sequence of cold, wet years. The rains smashed down from an iron sky onto the fields of France, bending ears of wheat, retarding growth, rotting the grain before it could be brought in from the field, so that even . . . at harvest time, people were hungry. The

is also possible that he was not a werewolf but a serial killer and cannibal. Another theory is that Stubbe was none of the above. Rather, he may have been an unfortunate pawn in a religious war between Catholics and Protestants. During the period of

poor and starving were everywhere. . . .
Men and women, young and old, shiv-
ered in the streets, skin hanging and
stomachs swollen. Others lay stretched
out in final exhaustion, the remains of a
desperate last meal of grass sticking out
of their mouths. . . . Sensitive observers
. . . were frankly shocked to see how
quickly hunger reduced the standards of
their fellow men to those of brute animals. Having no bread or other food, the
ravening peasants were reported to fall
on dead horses, asses, or any other carri-
on, leading one churchman to note that
"the pasturage of wolves has become the
food of Christians."

Adam Douglas, *The Beast Within.* London: Chapmans, 1992, p. 127.

Stubbe's alleged crimes, the Bedburg area was the central battle-
ground in this war. Stubbe, a member of a prominent Protestant
family, lived in a region dominated by Catholics. Some experts
believe that charges of lycanthropy were leveled at Stubbe, and

the pamphlet published, by religious leaders seeking to demonstrate their power and also as a warning to other Protestants.

The Stench Was Beyond Description

The battles between Protestants and Catholics in western Europe lasted until the mid-1600s. But werewolves continued to threaten the populace long after the religious wars ended. In fact, the worst werewolf epidemic in France appears to have occurred more than a century later. And it did not happen in a single town or region but throughout a 50 by 56 mile (80 by 90k) stretch of barren mountains and valleys in south-central France known as Gévaudan.

On June 30, 1764, a vicious, wolflike creature with reddish fur claimed its first victim, Jeanne Boulet, killed outside the village of Les Hubacs near Langogne. During the course of the next 5 months, the creature, given the name Wild Beast of Gévaudan, was said to have devoured 11 people, including 2 armed men. Unlike most werewolves, the beast did not stalk its prey far from town in the dead of night. In one brazen attack, a woman was carried off from her backyard garden in broad daylight. Summers describes the Wild Beast: "Its teeth were most formidable. With its immense tail it could deal swinging blows. It vaulted to tremendous heights, and ran with supernatural speed. The stench of the brute was beyond description."[47] But even worse than the smell was the manner in which the beast killed. It grabbed its victims and ripped off their faces with its razor-sharp teeth.

The death toll quickly grew to 50 as peasants tried to figure out the creature's true identity. Some believed it was a either a wild monkey or a hyena that had escaped from a local circus. Others said it was the mythical abominable snowman, the hideous off-

A series of brutal killings in south-central France in the mid-1700s was blamed on a vicious wolflike creature. While many came to believe the creature was a werewolf, others speculated that it might be the mythical abominable snowman (pictured).

spring of a bear and a wolf. A local bishop wrote a letter saying the beast was God's punishment, a warlock unleashed to punish the sinners of Gévaudan. As rumors multiplied, many came to believe the creature was a werewolf.

In January 1765 the story took a new turn when a child named Jacques Portefaix and 6 friends, including 2 young girls, fought off an attack by the wild beast. They drove the creature into the hills. King Louis XV heard about their brave deed and took a personal interest in the case. He awarded the group a large sum of money and promised to pay for the education of Portefaix. Following the event the king ordered armed infantry men, called dragoons, to the area to hunt down the wild beast.

By April 1765 most people in France had heard of the Wild Beast and its fearsome activities. The popular *Gazette de France* carried weekly stories about attacks and sightings. As public interest grew, engravers produced a series of shocking woodcuts that showed a large werewolf attacking helpless maidens or battling brave dragoons. Despite the attention of the French army, the number of attacks continued to increase, leading residents of Gévaudan to call the years between 1765 and 1767 the time of death. Parish records from those years show that the main victims were housewives and children.

The killings finally came to an end on June 19, 1767, when a nobleman called the Marquis d'Apcher organized a posse of several hundred men. After several days on the hunt, the men succeeded in surrounding the Beast of Gévaudan in a forest near Mont Mouchet. As dusk fell a local innkeeper named Jean Chastel was separated from the other men. He pulled out his Bible and began to read but looked up at some point and saw a giant werewolf walking toward him. He lifted his double-barrel musket and fired at the creature. This only enraged the beast, who charged at Chastel at full speed. The innkeeper fired another bullet into the creature's heart and it fell dead. Later Chastel said that he had used silver bullets made from melting down a medal of the Virgin Mary.

Although the Beast of Gévaudan did not revert to human form upon death, members of the large hunting party claimed the beast was half man, half wolf. Whether or not the creature was truly a werewolf, the death toll was high. An estimated 210 people were attacked and 113 had died, and of those victims, 98 were fully or partially eaten. Nearly two-thirds of the dead were children, while 25 were women and 6 were men. Some historians believe the attacks were perpetrated by a pack of particularly vicious wild wolves. However, as Woodward writes, "to the local population, who were appalled by the creature's trail of depredation and superhuman savagery, it was quite simply a werewolf. Certainly no other story since then has so assuredly caught the imagination of the French man-in-the-street."[48]

"Give Me Raw Meat!"

The widespread European fear of werewolves began to fade during the nineteenth century. While peasants in isolated villages might profess belief in the creatures, werewolfism largely moved into the realm of ancient superstition. Fairy tales like the 1813 "Little Red Riding Hood," with its big, bad wolf, kept the idea of child-eating wolf men alive, but werewolf sightings diminished significantly.

By the mid-1800s doctors came to understand that people who thought they were werewolves were suffering from a rare psychiatric disorder called lycanthropia, or clinical lycanthropy. This condition was reported in 1852 by a French patient being treated by a physician referred to by Woodward as Dr. Morel:

Fear of werewolves faded in Europe in the nineteenth century but fairy tales such as "Little Red Riding Hood" kept alive the idea of wolves that steal and eat children.

"See this mouth [the victim touches his lips] it is the mouth of a wolf; these are the teeth of a wolf. I have cloven feet; see the long hairs that cover my body and my paws. Let me run away into the woods so that you may shoot me there! . . . Give me raw meat! . . . I am a wolf, a wolf!"[49]

While clinical lycanthropy was first recognized as a mental disorder in ancient Greece, in the centuries that followed, those who suffered with the condition were usually executed. However, the case of Anton Léger shows how attitudes were changing in the nineteenth century. Léger believed himself to be a wolf. He moved from his father's house in Versailles, France, into the woods, where he set up a wolf lair in a cave. In 1824 the delusional man lured a young girl to his lair, killed her, and ate her. When he was captured and brought to trial, however, he was not executed like so many before him. Instead Léger was diagnosed with clinical lycanthropy and committed to a psychiatric hospital.

The Morbach Monster

By the twentieth century, werewolf sightings dropped off considerably. Most werewolves were seen only in movie theaters or on television screens. The creatures did not disappear entirely, however. Werewolves, including one known as the Morbach Monster, seemed to have found a home in the forests of Germany. Morbach is a munitions site for Hahn Air Force Base, just outside of the village of Wittlich. The fearsome Morbach Monster was seen there by U.S. airmen in 1988, but the first sighting dates back to 1812. At that time a French soldier named Schwytzer broke in to a farmhouse to steal food. After the soldier killed the farmer who lived there, the farmer's wife, who witnessed the crime, placed a curse on him. She chanted that Schwytzer should turn into a rabid wolf whenever the moon was full. The soldier killed the woman, but her curse took hold. During the next full moon, Schwytzer became a rapacious werewolf, killing and eating livestock, wildlife, and human beings.

Eventually, local residents found Schwytzer living deep in the

"[He] ate the brains out of his head as a most savory and dainty delicious meal to staunch his greedy appetite."

—A 1601 pamphlet describing the crimes of Peter Stubbe.

The Beast of Bray Road has been stalking the woods and fields of Wisconsin since 1936.

woods. They cornered him and killed him near Morbach. Later, townsfolk erected a shrine on the site to thank God for helping them dispose of the werewolf. A candle was placed in one of the windows, and local legend stated that as long as a candle remained lit, the werewolf would not return.

The candle reportedly went out one night in 1988 when a group of U.S. military personnel was driving by the shrine. A few men, aware of the legend, joked that they might see a werewolf that night. Several hours later, guards at the air base heard the ringing of an alarm coming from a portion of fence in a remote corner of the installation. When they investigated, one of the guards saw a huge, wolf-like animal stand up on its hind legs, stare at him for a few seconds, and jump over the tall, chain-link fence. When security forces brought their trained dogs to the site to search for the creature, the dogs began barking uncontrollably. Almost 10 years later, in 1997, an anonymous airman at the base contacted folklore researcher D.L. Ashliman to confirm the story:

> I was stationed at Hahn Air Base, Germany, from May 1986 to August 1989 as a security policeman, and it was my group that witnessed the Morbach Werewolf. . . . The creature that we saw was definitely an animal and definitely . . . wolf like. It was about seven to eight feet tall, and it jumped a twelve-foot security fence after taking three long leaping steps.[50]

Some speculate that the Morbach Monster is a distant relative of Schwytzer. They believe he reproduced and that his werewolf spawn continue to search for human flesh in the forests of Morbach.

The Beast of Bray Road

It is unknown if werewolves are immortal or even if they reproduce. Residents of southeastern Wisconsin have reported werewolf sightings on highways and in cornfields near the area of Delavan and Elkhorn for more than 70 years. Either the beast is very old or it has children and grandchildren living in the woods of Wisconsin.

One of the earliest of these sightings occurred in 1936, when Mark Schackelman saw a creature about the size of a man but with long, shaggy fur and the face of a German shepherd or wolf. He described it as a "demon straight from hell."[51] The wolf man of Wisconsin remained a quiet local legend until 55 years later. On December 31, 1991, Linda S. Godfrey, a reporter for the *Delavan Week*, spoke to a witness who said he saw something big, hairy, and wolf-like on Bray Road, a few miles outside of Elkhorn. Godfrey wrote a story called "The Beast of Bray Road," and the name stuck. After the article was published, many more people came forth to claim they had seen the creature. Since that time, Godfrey has heard of over 70 similar sightings.

Witnesses most often see the creature at night or in the early morning hours, between 10:30 P.M. and 5:00 A.M. It is usually spotted in cornfields between August and October, when the tall plants provide cover for the beast. Although it is said to be tall, furry, and threatening, no one has ever been hurt by the Wisconsin werewolf. Small game and deer seem to be its favorite prey, but it also eats roadkill and other dead creatures.

A typical sighting of the Beast of Bray Road took place in 2004, on October 30—the night before Halloween. On that night, an unnamed 45-year-old woman who worked as a registered nurse thought it would be fun to take her 14-year-old daughter and a friend for a drive in hopes of spotting the creature. Around 8:30 P.M. they were driving slowly near Bray Road when the beast stepped out of a cornfield and gave them a menacing look. The occupants of the car all screamed, and the woman pressed the gas pedal to the floor in hopes of making a quick escape. Later she described what she saw:

> It was covered in fur, with heavier fur on its back. It was dark in color but tipped silvery gray. It was in the oncoming lane of traffic so we were less than nine feet away, max. It was not a person in a suit, it was way too tall (about seven feet) way too brawny, and its eyes were glittery and dark, they had no . . . whites like a human eye in a mask would have. Its head was big, almost too big for its body. It had an elongated snout, but pointy, not rounded like a Lab's.
>
> It stood there, and then it hunched over into an aggressive stance. Its arms were bent at the elbow and forward. I couldn't see the hands. Its ears were pointed, shaped like a German shepherd's, but laid back. . . . It was looking right at me. I felt it was aggressive and would defend itself viciously.[52]

Werewolves continue to find a place in human imagination. In movies such as the popular 1981 film An American Werewolf in London *(pictured), in the hugely successful Harry Potter books and movies, in comic books, and in graphic novels, werewolves transform from human to beast and back again—terrifying and fascinating each new generation.*

The witnesses had a camcorder and a digital camera, but they were too frightened to take pictures. This seems to be the case with other similar reports about the Beast of Bray Road.

Although Wisconsin's werewolf remains elusive, the creature has received a great deal of media attention. Two Milwaukee television stations have run various stories about the beast, and a low-budget horror film called *The Beast of Bray Road* came out in 2006. In addition, the Beast of Bray Road was the subject of at least two books, *The Beast of Bray Road: Tailing Wisconsin's Werewolf* and *Hunting the American Werewolf.*

In centuries past, people were riveted by pamphlets covering the evil deeds of Peter Stubbe and newspapers reporting on the Wild Beast of Gévaudan. Today people continue to be fascinated with werewolves in their midst.

CHAPTER 4

Stopping Werewolf Attacks

In 1541 a farmer was arrested near Padua, Italy, for having viciously mutilated and eaten a number of people in the region. The man said he was not guilty and blamed the killings on a rabid wolf. However, local authorities were convinced that the man committed the crimes, and they thought they had a way to find out. It was commonly believed at the time that when werewolves were in human form, they had fur growing inside their bodies. In order to judge the farmer's guilt or innocence, authorities cut off his arms and legs searching for wolf hair under the flesh. Since the man was free of inner fur, he was deemed innocent. However, he soon died of blood loss and shock.

Barbarous acts like the one committed against the Italian farmer have a long history in Europe. For no technique was deemed too brutal or bloody to exterminate the wolfish blight upon humanity.

Hunting Werewolves

Whenever werewolf hysteria swept through a town or district, residents organized hunting parties to track and kill the monster responsible for the depredations. Since it was believed that werewolves possessed supernatural predatory skills and superhuman strength, hunters had to be well armed.

In addition to guns, swords, axes, and knives, werewolf trackers required special gear to kill their prey. These tools are similar to those used on vampires, since they are closely associated with werewolves in many countries. For example, in eastern Europe it is believed that werewolves and vampires can both be killed by driving a wooden stake through the heart. But extra measures are often taken for werewolves, because it is said they can regenerate destroyed heart tissue. Therefore, werewolf killers often cut the heart from the chest and burn it to ashes in a fire. Similarly, in cases where the creature is killed by smashing its skull, the head is removed and burned separately from the body to ensure its destruction.

Another method for destroying werewolves involves decapitation with a shovel. The instrument cannot be a standard shovel used in the garden but one used to dig graves in a churchyard. As parapsychologist Rosemary Ellen Guiley explains: "A grave digger's shovel possesses a certain supernatural potency from its association with the dead. A sexton's [churchyard caretaker's] shovel possesses the holy power of God."[53]

While silver in the form of knives or bullets can kill a vampire, the effect of silver on a werewolf is less certain. Some say a werewolf will die instantly after being shot with a pure silver bullet or being stabbed by a silver dagger, sword, or spear. Others say that this is a misconception based on the eighteenth-century

Did You Know?

It is believed that both werewolves and vampires can be killed by a wooden stake driven through the heart.

story about the Beast of Gévaudan, who was supposedly killed by silver bullets. However, according to ancient legend, German children wore small silver bells to protect against wolf and werewolf attacks. And in centuries past the Irish believed that werewolves could be repelled by wearing a wolf-tooth necklace made from silver. While silver talismans were worn for protection, they might have given rise to the idea that silver bullets and swords were harmful to werewolves.

Charms for Keeping Werewolves Away

Teeth were among the many body parts of the wolf that were used as protection against werewolves. In eighth-century Great Britain, the warrior Ceolwulf heard the unearthly screeching of werewolves in the night and was said to remark, "I have no fear . . . I have a wolf's snout hung around my neck and no [werewolf] can hurt me, be [its] charms ever so powerful."[54]

Wolf charms were also used to safeguard livestock. In 1550 Italian scientist Girolamo Cardano wrote that the tail of a wolf, when hung in a stable, would protect horses and oxen from being devoured. The paws and coat of the creature were also said to offer protection against werewolves.

Other werewolf repellents come from the plant kingdom. Rye grain is believed to have magical properties that will nullify a werewolf's supernatural powers. Mistletoe is another powerful herb, long associated with good luck. In Germany, Bulgaria, Romania, and Russia, peasants hung the leaves and berries over their doors and windows to prevent werewolves from entering the home.

Another herb, wolfsbane, as its name implies, is the bane of wolves. Also called aconite or monkshood, it was believed by the

Greeks to grow from the saliva of Cerberus, the three-headed dog guardian of the underworld. In later centuries wolfsbane was used to identify werewolves. If the flower cast a yellow shadow on a suspect's chin, it was a sign that he or she was a true werewolf. In addition, it is said that wolfsbane gives off an odor that greatly irritates the werewolf due to the creature's enhanced sense of smell.

Self-Imposed Prevention Measures

Preventive measures have at times been self-imposed—both as protection for unwitting victims and to keep the beast's condition secret. Accounts of werewolves building fortresses in which to hide at sunset or on nights when the moon is full have appeared in some books and other sources. During this time of transformation, a werewolf can lock itself in an unlit basement and fling the key into the darkness. The theory goes that by the time it finds the key, daylight will be upon the land and the werewolf will revert back to human form. Another method might involve securing doors with complicated combination locks. A human would understand how to unlock such devises, but the locks would defeat the beast's mind during lycanthropic episodes. In such cases windows and doors would have to be barred so that the creature could not break out with its superhuman strength.

The werewolf might have an accomplice—a child, a spouse, or a servant—that could lock it up during times of transformation. But as paranormal researcher Basil Cooper writes in *The Werewolf*, "all these measures, elaborate as they may seem, were but temporary palliatives; a slender barrier between the victim and ultimate discovery."[55] For this reason werewolves have long sought medicinal cures for their condition.

Cures for Werewolves

Some of those hoping to cast off their lycanthropy sought the help of doctors whom they believed could destroy the wolf part of their nature while leaving their humanity intact. As long ago as the seventh century, a bloody, painful method to cure lycanthropy was described by Greek surgeon Paul of Aegina. In the book *De Re Medica Septem*, Paul advises doctors they can cure werewolves at the time of attack by "opening a vein and abstracting blood to [cause] fainting, and giving the patient a diet of wholesome food."[56] Afterward, Paul recommends baths in sugar water and milk whey for three days. This is followed by causing the werewolf to vomit using a potion made from pulverized snakes, thyme, wormwood, vinegar, aloe, and other substances. Finally, the nostrils were to be rubbed with opium every night before bed.

Several cures focused on the forehead based on the belief that werewolves are particularly vulnerable between the eyes. Eleventh-century Arab physician Avicenna recommended branding the beast's forehead with a red-hot iron. A cure from Sicily advised administering a sharp blow to the forehead with a knife. As the blood flowed from the wound, it was said that the spirit of the wolf would flow from the body as well. Summers describes the case of a wealthy Italian nobleman who was freed from his werewolfism by this cure:

> It so chanced that at one [full moon] when the werewolf was scouring the midnight streets, there encountered him in his hot chase a young gallant, who . . . drew his [sword] and slashed the foul grinning monster, whose white fangs had already

snapped to bite, criss-cross over the slanting forehead. There gushed out great drops of black blood, thick like [tar], the [werewolf] uttered a long discordant howl of agony, his limbs convulsed, and there broke through [from] the animal the man, whom the juvenal [youth] recognized as one of his near and most honored friends. Since that happy encounter, and owing to the courage of the youth, the . . . lycanthrope was never again attacked by his lupine frenzy, but was thenceforth freed from the evil spell.[57]

This cure was said to work because it caused the blood to run black and thick, carrying away the werewolf's dark affliction. A similar cure could be accomplished by piercing the backs of the werewolf's hands with nails or knives.

Releasing the Afflicted Through Exorcism

Survival of such cures, especially those that involved deep cuts on the forehead, was by no means assured. For this reason, some favored exorcism, the ritualistic casting out of demons, as a means of separating the voracious wolf from its human host.

The word *exorcism* is derived from the Greek *exorkizein*, which means "to cause someone to swear." Technically, an exorcism does not drive the devil out of a person. Rather, the ritual makes the demon swear an oath, or allegiance, to the exorcist. This allows the person performing the ceremony to control or command the spirit to leave. As Christian bishop Demetrianus wrote in the third century A.D., after the exorcist administers spiritual blows, "the demons, screeching and yowling, are compelled to abandon the bodies they have so foully invaded, and release the afflicted from their travail and pain."[58]

Exorcism is mentioned many times in the Bible. By the 1500s, when suspected werewolves were being burned at the stake, exorcism and demon possession were well-established ideas in Christianity. According to the authors of *The Witch's Hammer*, exorcism "will disperse all glamour and objectively restore to human shape those upon whom an evil spell of fascination and metamorphosis has been cast."[59]

According to the New Testament, any baptized Christian can perform an exorcism. But no matter what their training or background, exorcists perform difficult, dangerous jobs when attempting to cast a werewolf demon out of a person's body. As the 1614 exorcism instruction book the *Roman Ritual* states, the exorcist is dealing with "an ancient and astute adversary, strong, and exceedingly evil" and the exorcist must have "a lively faith, an absolute confidence in God and Jesus."[60]

Werewolf exorcisms were often dramatic and frightening. Victims were sprinkled with holy water, which often brought forth hysterical fits, howls, and violent convulsions. The exorcist prayed for hours and loudly recited scriptures. Sometimes werewolves tried using their magical powers to escape. This required exorcists to lock doors and even nail boards over windows. Many times physical restraints such as straitjackets, ropes, or leather straps were necessary to immobilize the victim and prevent violence.

Spittle Flying, Eyes Wild

While most people associate werewolf exorcisms with the distant past, in 1992 Bishop Robert McKenna conducted an exorcism on Bill Ramsey, who was allegedly possessed by the demon of a werewolf. The exorcism was attended by four off-duty police officers meant to protect McKenna from the werewolf's attacks. Demonologists Ed and Lorraine Warren were also present, along with a newspaper journalist and a writer from *People* magazine.

According to reports of the exorcism, Ramsey became extremely agitated the moment he walked into the church for the exorcism. He was placed in a chair facing the altar, and McKenna approached him, demanding the werewolf demon within Ramsey identify itself. After 30 minutes of praying and ordering the werewolf to be banished, McKenna touched the stole he was wearing to Ramsey's forehead. This caused Ramsey to writhe, shake, and tremble violently. Suddenly, the werewolf took control and Ramsey's lips pulled back, revealing sharp, glistening teeth. His hands became claws and he took a violent swipe at the bishop's face. The police officers jumped up to restrain Ramsey, but the bishop ordered them away. McKenna then touched his crucifix to Ramsey's forehead. Ed and Lorraine Warren describe what happened next:

> Bill, or more properly, the werewolf inside him, went berserk. He came up from his chair snarling and growling and grasping at the Bishop. This time the Bishop had no choice but to retreat beyond the altar gate. Bill, spittle flying from his mouth, eyes wild, began to rush through the gate for the Bishop. But the priest stood absolutely still now, holding his cross up once again and beginning to speak in Latin. And then something happened. Bill felt suddenly weak; he staggered back to his chair and threw himself in it. He could feel the coldness

in his body begin to warm and he felt his desire to attack the Bishop begin to fade. . . .

Bill could feel the spirit of the werewolf within himself, and its desire to destroy the religious man. But the werewolf's power was slipping quickly away. A faint roar sounded in Bill's chest, and then faded. He brought up his hand[s], but they were no longer claw like. They were merely hands.[61]

"Crunching and Cracking of Bones"

Although exorcisms are traditionally a religious ritual, some werewolf exorcisms are not based on traditional religious practices. Some exorcists instead use magic spells that are as complicated and unusual as those that may have created the werewolf in the first place. In 1912 O'Donnell described werewolves in the Orenburg region in southern Russia and an exorcism performed to cure them.

The story concerns Tina Peroviskei, a wealthy young widow with three children who married a wealthy landowner named Ivan Baranoff. Because of the cold Russian climate, no one thought it unusual that Baranoff dressed from head to toe in gray furs, including fur leggings, hats, and coats. The widow thought him handsome, with bright, glossy hair and a set of large, gleaming white teeth. However, Peroviskei's relatives were frightened by her husband's cruel eyes and single, dark eyebrow. Peroviskei's children shrank from Baranoff's touch, even though he doted on them and constantly fed them rich, fatty foods.

Peroviskei started to have doubts about her marriage when her husband took to disappearing without a word between dusk and sunrise. When he returned in the morning, he would not tell

Exorcisms are most often associated with efforts to break a demon's hold on an innocent person, as is depicted in this painting from around 1300. Such rituals have also been used against werewolves.

her where he had been. She noticed drops of blood on his face and dried blood under his fingernails. Before long, Peroviskei's 4 beloved dogs disappeared on 4 consecutive nights. Each was found in the morning ripped asunder by a wolf. Soon after, the children were brutally attacked by 3 shadows in the night as Peroviskei cowered in terror in the next room. As O'Donnell describes it, 1 of the children shrieked and cried out for her mother, "then a series of savage snarls and growls and more shrieks—the combined shrieks of all three children. Shrieks and growls were then mingled together in one dreadful, hideous pandemonium, which all of a sudden ceased and was succeeded by the loud crunching and cracking of bones."[62]

Magical Exorcism

Peroviskei managed to escape by jumping from a window. She made her way into the town of Orsk, where she told her story to a friend in the military, Colonel Majendie. The colonel was accompanied by a priest, Reverend Rappaport, who told her that Baranoff and his two servants had long been suspected of lycanthropy. Majendie wanted to round up some soldiers, apprehend the werewolves, and kill them. But Rappaport asked if he could conduct a magical exorcism. The colonel replied, "You may exorcize the devils first. . . . We will hang and quarter the brutes afterwards."[63]

After a desperate, bloody struggle, Majendie and several soldiers managed to capture and secure Baranoff and his servants. Rappaport then proceeded with an exorcism that combined sorcerer's spells, astrology, and herbal potions. It was a black magic spell in reverse, meant to cast off the phantom of the Unknown that inhabited the werewolves.

Rappaport drew two circles on the ground in white chalk. Inside the inner circle he drew the astrological symbol for the planet Mercury inside a triangle. Mercury is said to be an opponent of evil spirits, and its position in the sky at the time of

"[Exorcism] will disperse all glamour and objectively restore to human shape those upon whom an evil spell of fascination and metamorphosis has been cast."

—*The Witch's Hammer.*

the ceremony was favorable to casting out devils. As O'Donnell explains, "In exorcism, as well as in the evocation of spirits, great attention must be paid to the position of the stars, as astrology exercises the greatest influence on the spirit world."[64]

After drawing a complex astrological formula on the ground, Rappaport surrounded the outer circle with lamps burning olive oil. He built an altar of wood and ordered the soldiers to build a fire in the inner circle. Over the flames, they placed a tripod holding an iron pot filled with spring water. Rappaport then prepared an herbal mixture with sulfur, opium, ammonia, camphor, asafetida, and other ingredients. He placed this in the pot along with a portion of mandrake root, a live snake, two live toads in linen bags, and some fungus. Next the exorcist constructed a magic wand, binding together ash, birch, and white poplar sticks. O'Donnell picks up the story:

> He next proceeded to pray, kneeling in front of the altar; and continued praying till the unearthly cries of the toads announced the fact that the water, in which they were immersed, was beginning to boil. Slowly getting up and crossing himself, he went to the fire, and dipping a cup in the pot, solemnly approached the werewolves, and slashing them severely across the head with his wand, dashed in their faces the seething liquid, calling out as he did so: "In the name of Our Blessed Lady I command thee to depart. Black, evil devils from hell, begone! Begone! Again I say Begone!" He repeated this three times to the vociferous yells of the werewolves, who struggled so frantically that

they succeeded in bursting their bonds, and, leaping to their feet, endeavored to escape into the bushes.[65]

The werewolves were pursued by the soldiers, and 1 was shot. As he died, he did not transform into a human but into a huge gray wolf. The other 2 were eventually tracked to a cave in the woods, where they were found with the half-eaten remains of an old woman and 2 children. The werewolves were shot, and they also transformed into regular wolves upon death. Peroviskei tore down Baranoff's mansion and built a new home on the site. However, to this day the newer home is said to be haunted by werewolves and the ghosts of the widow's 3 devoured children.

Reciting Spells

Rituals similar to the one performed by Rappaport have long been practiced in other parts of Europe. In eastern Germany accused werewolves were whipped with bundles of ash sticks until their entire bodies were bloody. As they cowered on the floor, boiling potions consisting of tar, vinegar, and various herbs were repeatedly poured over their bodies, sometimes for hours. Woodward provides a magical exorcism spell from that region that sounds like a nursery rhyme:

> Greywolf ugly, Greywolf old,
> Do at once as you are told.
> Leave this man and fly away,
> Where 'tis night and never day. . . .
> Away, away, shoo, shoo, shoo!

Exorcism Can Be a Beautiful Thing

From the 1940s until her death in 1985, British psychic Rose Gladden conducted dozens of exorcisms for people suffering from lycanthropy. Her healing technique combined traditional religious beliefs with modern New Age spiritual teachings. In an interview with Ian Woodward, Gladden explained attitudes toward werewolf exorcisms:

> I know from experience that a person cannot be possessed by these lower forces [of lycanthropy] unless he himself happens to be a low, evil type of person.

Do you think we care for you?
We'll whip thee again, with a crack, crack, crack!
Scourge thee and beat thee til thou art black;
Fool of a graywolf, we have thee at last,

Well, assuming he wants to be helped, I would try to uplift him spiritually, I would try to fight, on his behalf, whatever evil influences are troubling him. I would get him to try and understand God and the higher nature of man. . . . The light exists within all men, no matter how "bad" they are; they still have this tiny light. In the case of the lycanthrope, it is true, it may be extinguished; but I would help him to brighten it. Once it has brightened again, once it is shining out, the evil around him will dissolve and he will be ultimately cleansed. Exorcism, when it works, can be a beautiful thing.

Ian Woodward, *The Werewolf Delusion*. New York: Paddington, 1970, p. 146.

Back to thy hell home, out of him fast!. . .
We'll scratch thee, we'll prick thee,
We'll prod thee, we'll scald thee.
Fast, fast, out of him, fast![66]

After the beatings and scaldings, the werewolf was left on the floor. The demon spirit was expected to leave in the middle of the night, never to return. If the victim recovered from his or her wounds, it was said that his or her mood would be happy and bright for the rest of his or her life.

Spoiling the Blood

It is unknown when the last brutal werewolf exorcisms were conducted in Europe, although the practice was recorded in the early twentieth century. In the Caribbean island nation of Haiti, where some inhabitants practice voodoo, werewolf exorcisms were still taking place in the late twentieth century. Specifically, they involved werewolf-vampires that kill children.

Voodoo is a religion originally practiced by Haitian slaves that mixes ancient African tribal beliefs with Roman Catholic rituals and practices. Practitioners of voodoo believe in the existence of gods and goddesses, called *loa*. While many *loa* are positive, beneficial spirits, Haiti is said to be plagued with evil *loa*. Among these malevolent spirits are werewolves, or loup-garou as they are known by the French-speaking Haitians. These spirits are said to enter the bodies of magicians and sorceresses and suck the blood from living babies. In 1959 sociologist Alfred Métraux described the transformation from witch to loup-garou through the use of voodoo magic:

A woman werewolf getting ready for a night outing . . . frees herself of her [human] skin by rubbing her neck, wrists, and ankles with a concoction of magic herbs. She hides her skin in a cool place—in a jar or near a pitcher—so that it will not shrink. Thus, stripped to the quick, the woman werewolf makes movements which have the effect of preparing her for the flight which she will shortly undertake. Flames spurt from her armpits and anus, turkey wings sprout from her back. She takes off through the thatch of her house.[67]

The werewolf flies through the countryside searching for children to devour. Villagers have learned many ways of thwarting the werewolf's hunt, however. One ritual takes place even before a child's birth. In a ceremony called "spoiling the blood," a pregnant woman drinks bitter coffee mixed with a strong alcoholic beverage called clairin, which is made from sugar cane. This is laced with a few drops of gasoline, which is supposed to make the baby's blood foul-tasting. After drinking the horrid concoction, the woman bathes in water that has been infused with garlic, chives, thyme, nutmeg, manioc, coffee, and clairin. Once the baby is born, he or she is passed through the smoke of a clairin-fueled fire. A voodoo priest conducting the ceremony asks the mother three times who wants the baby. She says, "I do,"[68] which affirms her ownership of the child.

In a variation of the "spoiling the blood" ceremony, babies are made to eat cockroaches fried in castor oil, syrup, nutmeg,

Werewolves

and garlic. Other newborns are said to be protected because their blood is naturally salty or bitter and therefore distasteful to werewolves. If a loup-garou accidentally drinks some of this blood, it will be seized with violent bouts of vomiting.

Tied to a Cross

The belief in blood-sucking werewolves is also prevalent in some parts of Brazil. And one of the oddest werewolf exorcisms in recent history occurred in the town of Rosário do Sul in southern Brazil.

In early 1978 a 16-year-old Catholic schoolgirl named Eliana Barbosa claimed she was having evil visions and dreams in which she was possessed by a werewolf. After confessing to a priest, Barbosa was ordered to drag a large cross 450 feet (137m) up a hillside. The cross was implanted in the ground, and the girl was tied to it with rope wrapped around her arms and legs. Barbosa hung on the cross as a crowd gathered around. Street vendors set up food stalls to serve the sightseers, who eventually numbered more than 5,000. The girl was eventually taken down after being symbolically crucified for 3 days. The exorcism failed, however, as Barbosa continued to suffer from werewolf possession.

Like so many others plagued by delusions of lycanthropy, Barbosa was treated in a sad and sadistic manner. But the fear of werewolves is so powerful that people engage in mock crucifixions, scalding, whipping, and even force-feeding fried cockroaches to babies. Such practices may look ludicrous to outsiders. But as long as the fierce and bloody spirits of wolves haunt the human psyche, those who feel they are living among werewolves will try anything to find some peace.

Opposite:
A cow is readied for sacrifice during a voodoo festival in Haiti. Voodoo practitioners in Haiti believe in the existence of many gods, goddesses, and spirits, including malevolent spirits that take the form of werewolves.

NOTES

Introduction: Horror in the Moonlight

1. Tonya, "Pack of Werewolves," Your True Tales, November 2006. http://paranormal.about.com.

2. Tonya, "Pack of Werewolves."

Chapter 1: The Ancient Beast

3. N.K. Sandars, *The Epic of Gilgamesh*. New York: Penguin, 1985, p. 86.

4. Ovid, "*Metamorphoses*, Book 1: 199–243," Mythology, 2004. www.mythology.us.

5. Quoted in Leslie A. Sconduto, *Metamorphoses of the Werewolf*. Jefferson, NC: McFarland, 2008, p. 11.

6. Sconduto, *Metamorphoses of the Werewolf*, p. 11.

7. Pliny, "*Natural History,* vol. 3," Internet Archive, 2009. www.archive.org.

8. Sabine Baring-Gould, *The Book of Werewolves*. New York: Causeway, 1973, pp. 39–40.

9. Quoted in Sconduto, *Metamorphoses of the Werewolf*, p. 130.

10. Sconduto, *Metamorphoses of the Werewolf*, p. 128.

11. Quoted in H. Sidky, *Witchcraft, Lycanthropy, Drugs and Disease*. New York: Peter Lang, 1997, p. 217.

12. Quoted in Montague Summers, "The Origin of the Vampire," Unicorn Garden, 2009. www.unicorngarden.com.

13. Adam Douglas, *The Beast Within*. London: Chapmans, 1992, p. 168.

14. Quoted in "*Wolf in Mythology, Cult of Wolf-Warrior, Werewolves,*" Cassiopaea, July 15, 2009, www.cassiopaea.org.

15. Quoted in Harry A. Senn, *Were-Wolf and Vampire in Romania*. Boulder, CO: Eastern European Monographs, 1982, p. 65.

16. Senn, *Were-Wolf and Vampire in Romania*, p. 2.

17. Quoted in Edward Sapir and Leslie

Sapir, eds., *Yale University Publications in Anthropology: Numbers Eight to Thirteen.* New Haven: Human Relations Area Files, 1970, p. 13.

18. Quoted in Sapir and Sapir, *Yale University Publications in Anthropology,* p. 26.

19. Quoted in Sapir and Sapir, *Yale University Publications in Anthropology,* pp. 18–19.

Chapter 2: From Human to Wolf

20. Elliot O'Donnell, *Werewolves.* New York: Longvue, 1965, p. 55.

21. O'Donnell, *Werewolves,* p. 56n.

22. Ian Woodward, *The Werewolf Delusion.* New York: Paddington, 1970, p. 117.

23. Quoted in Woodward, *The Werewolf Delusion,* pp. 114–15.

24. Quoted in Woodward, *The Werewolf Delusion,* p. 113.

25. Quoted in Montague Summers, *The Werewolf in Lore and Legend.* Mineola, NY: Dover, 2003, p. 292.

26. Quoted in Woodward, *The Werewolf Delusion,* pp. 115–16.

27. O'Donnell, *Werewolves,* p. 58.

28. Quoted in "Wolfstrap," Monstrous, 2009. http://werewolves.monstrous.com.

29. Summers, *The Werewolf in Lore and Legend,* p. 121.

30. Summers, *The Werewolf in Lore and Legend,* p. 112.

31. Quoted in D.L. Ashliman, "Werewolf Legends of Germany," University of Pittsburgh, 2002. www.pitt.edu.

32. Quoted in Woodward, *The Werewolf Delusion,* p. 120.

33. O'Donnell, *Werewolves,* p. 238.

34. Woodward, *The Werewolf Delusion,* pp. 128–29.

35. Quoted in Woodward, *The Werewolf Delusion,* p. 135.

36. J.A.L. Singh, "The Diary of the Wolf-Children of Midnapore (India)," Feral Children.com, 2009. www.feralchildren.com.

37. Singh, "The Diary of the Wolf-Children of Midnapore (India)."

38. Singh, "The Diary of the Wolf-Children of Midnapore (India)."

Chapter 3: Werewolves on the Prowl

39. Quoted in *Deseret News,* "Werewolf Hotline—346,000 Phone Calls," November 6, 1987, p. 20.

40. Quoted in Douglas, *The Beast Within,* p. 131.

41. Quoted in Sconduto, *Metamorphoses of the Werewolf*, p. 136.

42. Quoted in Charlotte F. Otten, ed., *A Lycanthropy Reader.* Syracuse: Syracuse University Press, 1986, p. 114n.

43. Quoted in Summers, *The Werewolf in Lore and Legend*, p. 229.

44. Quoted in Ashliman, "Werewolf Legends of Germany."

45. Quoted in Ashliman, "Werewolf Legends of Germany."

46. Quoted in Ashliman, "Werewolf Legends of Germany."

47. Summers, *The Werewolf in Lore and Legend*, p. 235.

48. Woodward, *The Werewolf Delusion*, pp. 223–24.

49. Quoted in Woodward, *The Werewolf Delusion*, p. 47.

50. Quoted in Ashliman, "Werewolf Legends of Germany."

51. Quoted in Linda S. Godfrey, "Wereblog April–May 2006," The Beast of Bray Road: Hunting the American Werewolf, 2006. www.beastofbrayroad.com.

52. Quoted in Linda S. Godfrey, "Creature Sightings Log," The Beast of Bray Road:

Hunting the American Werewolf, 2006. www.beastofbrayroad.com.

Chapter 4: Stopping Werewolf Attacks

53. Rosemary Ellen Guiley, *The Complete Vampire Companion.* New York: Macmillan, pp. 37–38.

54. Quoted in Summers, *The Werewolf in Lore and Legend*, p. 70.

55. Basil Cooper, *The Werewolf.* New York: St. Martin's, 1977, p. 36.

56. Quoted in Woodward, *The Werewolf Delusion*, p. 136.

57. Summers, *The Werewolf in Lore and Legend*, pp. 164–65.

58. Quoted in Summers, *The Werewolf in Lore and Legend*, p. 116.

59. Quoted in Summers, *The Werewolf in Lore and Legend*, p. 114.

60. Quoted in T.K. Oesterreich, *Possession, Demoniacal & Other.* Seacaucus, NJ: Citadel, 1966, p. 102.

61. Quoted in John Zaffis, "Bill Ramsey the Werewolf," Seekers of the Supernatural, March 14, 2009. http://seekersofthesupernatural.com.

62. O'Donnell, *Werewolves*, p. 85.

63. Quoted in O'Donnell, *Werewolves*, p. 88.

64. O'Donnell, *Werewolves*, p. 88.

65. O'Donnell, *Werewolves*, p. 90.

66. Quoted in Woodward, *The Werewolf Delusion*, pp. 142–43.

67. Quoted in C.S. Giscombe, "Natural Abilities & Natural Writing," Chain, Mills College, 2001. http://people.mills.edu.

68. Quoted in Woodward, *The Werewolf Delusion*, p. 144.

Books

Angela Cybulski, ed., *Werewolves.* San Diego: Greenhaven, 2004. Part of the Fact or Fiction? series, this book explores whether or not humans can transform themselves into werewolves. The topic is explored by experts in the fields of medicine, psychiatry, history, folklore, and magic.

Scott Francis, *Monster Spotter's Guide to North America.* Cincinnati: HOW Books, 2007. This book explores more than a hundred fascinating and terrifying monsters, including werewolves, that are said to be found in North America.

Linda S. Godfrey, *Werewolves.* New York: Checkmark, 2008. The journalist who first wrote about the Beast of Bray Road takes a look at the mystery of werewolves. This book features modern-day accounts from across the United States from eyewitnesses reporting on strange encounters with wolf-like creatures.

Rosemary Guiley, *The Encyclopedia of Vampires, Werewolves, and Other Monsters.* New York: Checkmark, 2005. A thorough compendium of monster tales and beliefs from all over the world and throughout history, including werewolves such as the Slavic *vlokolak* and the Shetland *wulver.*

Charlaine Harris and Toni L.P. Kelner, eds., *Wolfsbane and Mistletoe.* New York: Ace, 2008. This book features sad, funny, and scary tales of werewolves that appear during the Christmas holidays, written by best-selling masters of the horror genre.

Stephen Krensky, *Werewolves.* Minneapolis: Lerner, 2007. A book about werewolves, their habits, and their history. The last chapter features werewolf appearances in movies.

Web Sites

The Beast of Bray Road (www.beast ofbrayroad.com). This site is maintained by author Linda S. Godfrey, who has been reporting on a werewolf and other were-creatures seen around Elkhorn, Wisconsin. Godfrey maintains a blog and publishes recent eyewitness accounts and drawings said to be the werewolf of Wisconsin.

Feral Children (www.feralchildren. com). A Web site with stories about children who were allegedly raised by wolves. Includes the fascinating 41-page diary of the Reverend J.A.L. Singh, who discovered the wolf girls of Midnapore, India, in 1920.

Monstrous Werewolves (http://were wolves.monstrous.com). This site features extensive information about werewolves, along with drawings, photos, and links to other were-creatures such as weredogs and werecats.

The Werewolf in Literature (www. gwthomas.org/werewolfinliterature.htm). A catalog of werewolf writings from ancient Greece to graphic novels, with analyses, illustrations, and links to sources.

Werewolves (www.werewolves.com). This site provides wide-ranging information about werewolves, including transformations, hunting, films, vampires, werewolves, and clinical lycanthropy.

INDEX

ABOUT THE AUTHOR

Stuart A. Kallen is a prolific author who has written more than 250 nonfiction books for children and young adults over the past 20 years. His books have covered countless aspects of human history, culture, and science, from the building of the pyramids to the music of the twenty-first century. Some of his recent titles include *How Should the World Respond to Global Warming*, *Romantic Art*, and *Communication with the Dead.* Kallen is also an accomplished singer-songwriter and guitarist in San Diego, California.